Encounters with HCI Pioneers

A Personal History and Photo Journal

Synthesis Lectures on Human-Centered Informatics

Editor
John M. Carroll, *Penn State University*

Human-Centered Informatics (HCI) is the intersection of the cultural, the social, the cognitive, and the aesthetic with computing and information technology. It encompasses a huge range of issues, theories, technologies, designs, tools, environments, and human experiences in knowledge work, recreation and leisure activity, teaching and learning, and the potpourri of everyday life. The series publishes state-of-the-art syntheses, case studies, and tutorials in key areas. It shares the focus of leading international conferences in HCI.

Encounters with HCI Pioneers: A Personal History and Photo Journal
Ben Shneiderman

ISBN: 978-3-031-01096-5   Paperback
ISBN: 978-3-031-00204-5   Hardcover

DOI 10.1007/978-3-031-02224-1

A Publication in the Springer series
SYNTHESIS LECTURES ON HUMAN-CENTERED INFORMATICS, #41
Series Editor: John M. Carroll, Penn State University

Series ISSN: 1946-7680 Print   1946-7699 Electronic

Encounters with HCI Pioneers

A Personal History and Photo Journal

Ben Shneiderman
University of Maryland

SYNTHESIS LECTURES ON HUMAN-CENTERED INFORMATICS #41

ABSTRACT

The huge success of personal computing technologies has brought astonishing benefits to individuals, families, communities, businesses, and government, transforming human life, largely for the better. These democratizing transformations happened because a small group of researchers saw the opportunities to convert sophisticated computational tools into appealing personal devices offering valued services by way of easy-to-use interfaces. Along the way, there were challenges to their agenda of human-centered design by: (1) traditional computer scientists who were focused on computation rather than people-oriented services and (2) those who sought to build anthropomorphic agents or robots based on excessively autonomous scenarios. The easy-to-learn and easy-to-use interfaces based on direct manipulation became the dominant form of interaction for more than six billion people.

This book gives my personal history of the intellectual arguments and the key personalities I encountered. I believe that the lessons of how the discipline of Human-Computer Interaction (HCI) and the profession of User Experience Design (UXD) were launched can guide others in forming new disciplines and professions. The stories and photos of the 60 HCI pioneers, engaged in discussions and presentations, capture the human drama of collaboration and competition that invigorated the encounters among these bold, creative, generous, and impassioned individuals.

KEYWORDS

Human-Computer Interaction (HCI), User Experience Design (UXD), paradigm birth, research pioneers, direct manipulation

Contents

Introduction

The excitement of founding a new discipline brings together those with a shared vision that breaks from tradition. Success requires a motivated and determined community that values collaboration, even as individuals are pushing their own agendas and reputations. I've had the opportunity to see the energy and turmoil of those who contributed to the formation of Human-Computer Interaction (HCI), and the pleasure to see it succeed far beyond my expectations.

The book contains my personal reflections about the people I worked with and the ideas we wrestled with as we worked together to create theories, principles, guidelines, inspirational prototypes, and breakthrough ideas that were manifest in papers, journals, books, conferences, curricula, businesses, and much more.

The first three chapters are a partial personal history, with recollections of memorable encounters, influential contributors, and disconcerting controversies, as we built a new discipline in the 1970s, 1980s, and 1990s. A more complete description of my contributions are on my home page http://www.cs.umd.edu/~ben/about.html and in a timeline of my career http://www.cs.umd. edu/~ben/timeline.html. This book focuses on the HCI community's history, so I cite papers that describe our discipline's evolution.

I recognize that historians and my colleagues are likely to differ on whose ideas were influential, so I welcome their accounts. These multiple perspectives will enrich us all and inform new generations of students, historians, and journalists about our transformative contributions to the success of key technologies such as the World Wide Web, e-commerce, social media, and novel visual media, such as videos, artificial and virtual reality, and information visualization.

Chapter 4 discusses future possibilities for HCI. Chapter 5 describes the second component of this book, which are my photos and comments about 60 of the luminaries who contributed to the emergence of HCI. This set of people, whom I call HCI Pioneers, is based on my personal encounters and is therefore incomplete, as I describe in Chapter 5, with my sincere apologies to the many other people who also made important contributions. I hope that seeing the photos of individuals engaged in discussions and presentations helps capture the human drama of teamwork and competition that invigorated the encounters among these bold, creative, generous, and impassioned individuals.

Acknowledgments

I've had the pleasure of having a satisfying career filled with professional accomplishments, made meaningful by my personal connections with mentors, colleagues, and students. Catherine Plaisant has been a supportive colleague and close friend for more than 30 years, making my time at work satisfying, productive, and fun. My wife, Jennifer Preece, has been a loving partner, trusted advisor, and knowledgeable colleague who enriches my life in many ways every day. They both provided thoughtful comments and encouragement for this project.

I give warm thanks to Jeffrey Bigham, Sara Bly, Jack Carroll, Clarisse Sieckenuis de Souza, Alan Dix, Fan Du, Paul Dourish, Ernest Edmonds, Steven Feiner, Gerhard Fischer, Jim Foley, Jon Froehlich, Thomas Hewett, Jim Hollan, Bonnie John, Joe Konstan, Jonathan Lazar, Marilyn Mantei, Matt Mauriello, Judith S. Olson, Gary Perlman, Bernard Rous, Jean Scholtz, Markus Schmid, Loren Terveen, Ron Vetter, Ping Wang, Mark Anderson, and Clayton Lewis for constructive and supportive comments on drafts of this book, two articles on *Medium*, and one in *IEEE Computer*.

Special thanks to Gary Perlman for help with HCIBIB data (www.hcibib.org) and for creating the remarkable HCI Bibliography, which has been an important resource for our field. Thanks also to Matt Ericson for obtaining the *New York Times* data and Fan Du for preparing the charts. Deep appreciation to University of Maryland students Catherine Bloom, Sarah Sexton, and Gowtham Ashok who were excellent contributors in creating the HCI Pioneers website during 2016, although I did revisions at the end of 2018 for this publication. Rick Weisburd was instrumental in breaking my rare writing impasse by merging several unpublished essays into a coherent presentation, which laid the foundation for my further additions. Heartfelt thanks to Diane Cerra, Jack Carroll, and their team for working with me to bring this project to publication.

Part 1: A Personal History of HCI

CHAPTER 1

The Emergence of Human-Computer Interaction

Time it was, and what a time it was,
It was a time of innocence, A time of confidences.

Simon and Garfunkel, 1968

Young Human-Computer Interaction (HCI) researchers take for granted that their discipline is part of the academic landscape, but it wasn't always that way. The early days were turbulent times in which visionaries sought to break from existing traditions by proposing bold ideas. There are many origin myths for HCI with competing scenarios of how this discipline succeeded. It was a time of paradigm birth, more than paradigm shift, when pioneers were excited about how the emerging computing technology brought compelling new possibilities. I have tried to capture some of the stories of the generous and impassioned pioneers who laid the foundation for HCI. While the pioneers have different perspectives on whose work and which ideas were influential, there is a shared pride in having created a robust discipline, which continues to grow. As time goes by, historians will sift these stories to find durable truths; but for now, here is my version of how HCI began.

1.1   THE EARLY VISIONARIES: BUSH, LICKLIDER, ENGELBART

As World War II was drawing to an end, President Roosevelt's Science Adviser, Vannevar Bush (1890–1974), published the remarkable essay "As We May Think" in the July 1945 issue of *Atlantic Monthly*. He offered a vision of a new technology tool that would support scientists, lawyers, inventors, and other information-oriented professionals. His dream was of a desk-based personal machine that would provide rapid access to scientific papers, legal decisions, or patents. Bush's technology scenario was based on microfilm projection and electronics, but the key concept was the personal nature of this machine. He called his system "memex" for memory extender and had a rich understanding of the trails (links) that could connect one document to another. The memex concept predated digital computers, so his vision was based on microfilm technology with accompanying electronics to enable linking of documents and following of trails.

Bush's interface design was crude—typing the code number of the document was required to follow a link—but his concepts were compelling:

Wholly new forms of encyclopedias will appear, ready-made with a mesh of associative trails running through them, ready to be dropped into the memex and there amplified. The lawyer has at his touch the associated opinions and decisions of his whole experience, and of the experience of friends and authorities. . . . There is a new profession of trail blazers, those who find delight in establishing useful trails through the enormous mass of the common record. The inheritance from the master becomes, not only his addition to the world's record, but for his disciples the entire scaffolding by which they were erected.

Digital computers emerged in the following decade and so did the concepts of personal use. J. C. R. Licklider (1915–1990) was a quiet visionary more in touch with the digital possibilities. His essay "Man-Computer Symbiosis" (1960) envisioned powerful computers for personal use and a belief that voice recognition would be the common way to operate computers within five years. This essay had many forward-looking ideas and called for psychological studies, but he was promoting the image of computer as partner, not tool:

In the anticipated symbiotic partnership, men will set the goals, formulate the hypotheses, determine the criteria, and perform the evaluations. Computing machines will do the routinizable work that must be done to prepare the way for insights and decisions in technical and scientific thinking.

Figure 1.1: J. C. R. Licklider visits our group at the University of Maryland, April 1979.

While Licklider valued human capabilities, his message was seen as promoting equality and sometimes machine dominance. This distinction—between artificially intelligent machines that (or as promoters would say "who") could be our partners, tutors, or replacements and the tool-like user interface that empowers the user—is a repeated theme in this book. By the late 1960s, personal computing scenarios were common, but the distinction became a battle between those who promoted artificially intelligent machines on the one hand or tools to support or amplify human performance, on the other. Licklider visited our research group at the University of Maryland in April 1979 and then hosted me for a talk at MIT in October 1981.

Doug Engelbart (1925–2013) brought many ideas to reality during the 1960s with his grand dream of empowering and augmenting human intellect through advanced information technologies. Engelbart, through his Human Augmentation Center at the Stanford Research Institute, led the way by inventing and implementing new concepts such as early forms of hypertext links, cooperative work, windows, outliners, and a personal pointing device called the mouse. Engelbart's demo (1968) at the Fall Joint Computer Conference astonished viewers with his two-handed input and collaborative strategies, but Engelbart still felt that he lost the battle to the promoters of artificial intelligence (AI); he believed that they had a role in stopping funding for his human-centered ideas.

Figure 1.2: Doug Engelbart presenting at the ACM Hypertext Conference 1987.

Three decades would pass before Engelbart's work was properly acknowledged with the 1997 Turing Award of the Association for Computing Machinery (ACM). This award, often called the Nobel Prize of computing, is usually given to theoreticians and traditional computer scientists. I was part of the group that gave Engelbart a Special Recognition Award from the ACM Special Interest Group in Computer Human Interaction (SIGCHI) in 1998. The aging Engelbart tearfully accepted this and other awards: sweet victories after decades of being pushed aside. His bitterness was strongest against the AI visionaries from MIT: Marvin Minsky and John McCarthy.

The case for user interfaces was strengthened by Ivan Sutherland's Sketchpad system (1963), which opened the doors for graphical interaction and gestural input. Early reviews by Andries Van Dam (1966) and Charles Meadow (1970) helped stimulate interest in computer graphics, animation, and graphical user interfaces.

Psychological experiments on programming by batch vs. time sharing was an early hot topic in HCI (Grant and Sackman, 1967; Gold, 1969; Sackman, 1970), and the slow response of early time-sharing systems also led to several investigations (Carbonell, Elkind, and Nickerson, 1968; Miller, 1968).

Gerald Weinberg's (1933–2018) book (1971), *The Psychology of Computer Programming*, is a continuing inspiration to thinking about how people interact with computers. I might have liked the title better as the *Anthropology of Computer Programming*, but Jerry certainly made programming a lively human endeavor. My three-day visit to him at his Nebraska farm house remains a continuing stimulus to my work and personal life. Jerry's human-centered approach to studying programmers inspired my research and his independent thinking guided me in trusting my own beliefs. My review of programming studies at the National Computer Conference (1975) grew into the 1980 book *Software Psychology*.

James Martin (1933–2013) provided a thoughtful and useful survey of interactive systems in his book (1973), *Design of Man-Computer Dialogues*. He blended practical thinking and broad knowledge to create a useful guide for developers and researchers. Although Martin was enormously successful in the business world, his integrative capabilities were scorned in the academic community. I greatly appreciated James Martin's taking me into his world, inviting me to give a course at the IBM Systems Research Institute on Designing Effective Person/Computer Interfaces in July 1978, and then elsewhere in IBM. He returned the compliment by coming to speak in my June 1992 "User Interface Strategies" satellite TV show.

Figure 1.3: James Martin, two occasions approximately 1992.

Figure 1.4: Joseph Weizenbaum visits my University of Maryland office, April 26, 1982.

When Joseph Weizenbaum (1923–2008) demonstrated his ELIZA program (1966), which acted as a Rogerian therapist, many researchers believed that practical natural language systems and even effective psychotherapy were just around the corner. Weizenbaum was shocked by these responses, since his goal was to show how easily simple language exchanges could be implemented with 300 lines of LISP code.

Another 20 years would pass before user interface studies revealed the difficulties and showed the strength of alternatives. By contrast, human-human communications tools such as email, bulletin boards, and more sophisticated computer mediated conferencing systems have gone on to become dramatic successes. Pioneering systems, such as the Electronic Information Exchange System (EIES), were developed and studied by Roxanne Hiltz and Murray Turoff starting in the early 1970s (1978). Ted Nelson's visionary ideas about a vast docuverse were also ahead of their time and outside a familiar academic or commercial context (1973), but their descendants such as hypertext and the World Wide Web have become widespread.

Another important source of early human factors and HCI research was the celebrated community at Bell Labs in Murray Hill and Holmdel, New Jersey. Key people included Tom Landauer, Susan Dumais, Louis M. Gomez, George Furnas, and Judith Reitman Olson. Other centers were at IBM Research's T. J. Watson Labs in Yorktown Heights, NY, Digital Equipment Corporation in Maynard, MA, and Xerox's Palo Alto Research Center (PARC).

1.2   EMPIRICAL STUDIES AND GUIDELINES DOCUMENTS GAIN PROMINENCE

By the early 1970s things were moving along at many research centers but workers were largely isolated except when they could get together at conferences. The thirsty and isolated pioneers were eager to drink up new ideas and get a smile or hug of recognition. New systems were emerging and there was a rush to publish informal design guidelines based on experience. Fred Hansen was among the first (1971) and he coined the classic line "Know Thy User." John Bennett (1972), Tony Wasserman (1973), and James Foley and Victor Wallace (1974) were quick to follow with their own design guidelines. Stephen Engel and Richard Granda (1975) were more thorough and developed an influential guidelines document at IBM (1975), where Richard Hirsch was responsible for much early human factors work. Tom Sheridan at MIT was another human factors pioneer, who was famous for his work on control rooms (1974).

Alphonse Chapanis (1917–2002) began doing studies of interactive communication methods for team problem solving (1975). His rigorous and innovative work on technology-mediated cooperation was also beyond the acceptable psychology department agendas of his time. I shared an office with Chapanis in 1982, when we were both consultants to IBM working to increase usability efforts in projects such as air traffic control, the Global Positioning System, U.S. Navy sonar systems, and healthcare systems.

Figure 1.5: Alphonse Chapanis speaking at the May 1982 Gaithersburg, MD Conference.

During the mid-1970s, there were sporadic efforts to work on user interfaces, especially relating to the new thing of that era: time-shared computing that gave immediate responses to programmers. This was a great step forward over the punched card approach to preparing and submitting programs as large decks of cards. These programmer performance studies produced one of the many interesting and counter-intuitive results in human factors research. Programmers with immediate responses did not complete projects faster than those who worked with a three-hour delay. Long delays gave time and incentive to think carefully and get the program correct in a few tries. Immediate responses led to hasty thinking and much more debugging to correct mistakes. Researchers, including me, who were interested in psychological issues studied flowchart usage, meaningful variable names in programs, formatting, commenting strategies, and other supports for programmers.

But studies of programming and user interfaces were a side show. The AI community grabbed the journalist's attention and defense agency's funding; their promises of natural language translation and database query, voice recognition, and mobile robots were entrancing. Provocative doctoral dissertations and impressive demos gave the impression that researchers were close to solving the problems and making commercial products. Bill Woods' LUNAR answered natural language questions about the moon rocks from Apollo missions, Terry Winograd's SHRDLU understood and could use a robot arm to manipulate the micro-world of colored blocks of varying shapes, and the INTELLECT database query program went commercial. When I attended the first International Joint Conference on Artificial Intelligence in Washington, DC in 1977, excitement was high as delegates presented their papers and promises.

There were skirmishes between the practical implementer types and those pushing for more psychologically oriented research. The 1975 National Computer Conference brought these contrasts forward with a dramatic session on the emerging topic of database query languages. Advocates of these competing approaches presented their work in a session that I chaired. The IBM East Coasters offered a novel visual language called Query-by-Example (Zloof, 1975) and a thoughtful experiment (Thomas and Gould, 1975). The IBM West Coasters presented a comparative study of SEQUEL (later SQL) and SQUARE that clearly demonstrated the advantages of SEQUEL and also led to its refinement (Reisner, Boyce, and Chamberlin, 1975). While QBE was implemented commercially first, SQL became the dominant approach.

In England, at Loughborough University during the 1970s, Brian Shackel had been moving from research on human factors to user interfaces (Shackel, 1991). His colleague, Ken Eason, took a socio-technical systems approach in describing "the naïve computer user" (1976). In 1968, Brian Gaines furthered the case for research by starting the *International Journal of Man-Machine Studies* and developed early systems (Gaines and Facey, 1975). Eventually the journal was renamed the *International Journal of Human-Computer Studies*. At Sheffield University, under Max Sime's leadership, Thomas Green and D. J. Guest conducted influential basic research studies of cognitive aspects of programming (1973).

As interest grew in studies of programmers and database query languages, in 1975 I traveled to speak at the Universities of Utah, Massachusetts, Indiana, Minnesota, Wisconsin, Illinois, California-Berkeley, Ohio State, Purdue, and Virginia Polytechnic Institute and State University. Overall, I delivered more than 1,200 talks, including more than 100 keynotes. Early gatherings included the 1976 New York conference of the Human Factors Society on "The Role of Human Factors in Computers" (Shneiderman, 1976).

Government research also showed the tension between conducting psychological studies vs. implementation efforts that emphasized mission-driven software engineering. Richard Pew described his experience in creating a usability lab at the Social Security Administration outside Baltimore in 1978–1979. He built a strong research group that applied emerging HCI methods, but a new manager came in and cancelled the project, eliminated the lab, and disbanded the team (Pew, 2007).

Social concerns had been raised very early by Norbert Wiener (1950). Concerns increased as computers became the basis for widely used applications in business and government, leading Ted Sterling to describe key principles in thoughtful way for practitioners in the *Communications of the ACM* (1974).

In 1980, I published a book that reviewed the studies of programmers under the title *Software Psychology: Human Factors in Computer and Information Systems*. It focused on how to make programmers and database users more effective and closed with two chapters on interactive systems. The publisher thought this exotic book about the marriage of disciplines would sell only a couple thousand copies, but both of the popular computer science book-of-the-month clubs featured this book, which helped provoke interest in this obscure topic.

The interest in psychological studies of user interfaces as a separate topic continued to incubate in the early 1980s, but the birth of the new discipline was undoubtedly in March 1982 at Gaithersburg, MD. The Conference on Human Factors in Computing Systems grew out of the Washington, DC Software Psychology Society—an independent group started in 1976 that prided itself on its policy of "no members, no officers, and no dues." Despite its renegade nature, our 600-person mailing list announced monthly lectures that presented key speakers and drew 30–70 attendees (Shneiderman, 1986). Bill Curtis and I led the way in organizing the Gaithersburg conference, hoping to get 200 attendees for this new topic. After all, the Xerox STAR had been marketed for knowledge workers since 1981 and personal computers were being sold to more than just hobbyists. Command-line interfaces such as UNIX and DOS predominated, but windowing strategies and graphic user interfaces (GUIs) were already hot topics among the cognoscenti. The unanticipated interest in human factors led to 906 attendees, which fortunately could be accommodated in the auditoriums of the National Bureau of Standards (now the National Institute of Standards and Technology).

This heartening success of the Gaithersburg conference accelerated efforts to form a Special Interest Group on Computer Human Interaction (SIGCHI) within the ACM, leading to a November 1983 conference in Boston. Ironically, there was no SIGCHI Conference in 1984, the year of Big Brother, but the SIGCHI conference has been held annually since 1985 and now draws up to 4000 attendees. The annual CHI conference is the premier venue for user interface researchers and practitioners, but in addition, SIGCHI runs 30+ conferences a year on focused topics around the world.

The Gaithersburg conference gave me increased confidence about the importance of HCI research, so I sought to expand my efforts at the University of Maryland. I already had a modest grant from Control Data Corporation starting in January 1981 to study "Human Factors Research in Editor Interfaces" for the groundbreaking PLATO education system. Prof. Azriel Rosenfeld, a remarkable senior colleague who was a pioneer in computer vision, believed in my work enough to invite me to start the Human-Computer Interaction Lab (HCIL) in 1983 as part of his Center for Automation Research (Shneiderman, 1993a). This boost encouraged me to be more ambitious, leading me to propose and receive a larger grant from Control Data and a still bigger one from IBM to support the HCIL. The HCIL, which last year celebrated its 35th anniversary, remains one of my greatest satisfactions.

This vibrant community of people who work hard to support students and help each other succeed is now on its eighth director (Shneiderman et al., 2013). Its traditions include an annual symposium that draws 200+ paying participants leading us to require rehearsals, sometimes more than once, of every talk by faculty and students. Another key to HCIL's capacity to produce strong papers for the CHI and other conferences, was our internal reviews and paper clinics in which draft papers were vigorously discussed with the goal of helping authors to make better papers. For more than 30 years, Catherine Plaisant was my partner in running the lab, writing proposals, and doing great research. We have co-authored more than 100 papers, steadily building respect for each other as researchers, colleagues, and friends.

1.3   THE ORIGINS OF DIRECT MANIPULATION

My early interest in visual screen interaction led me to implement a lightpen-based graphic system for manipulating polynomials in 1972. I was amazed to see enthusiasm from high school students and computer science faculty who were engrossed by the capacity to point at polynomial coefficients on the screen and watch the curves expand, blossom, and oscillate across the display (Shneiderman, 1974).

There were many others who grasped the power of visual interfaces. Alan Kay and Adele Goldberg (1977) contributed to early work at Xerox Palo Alto Research Center (PARC) in developing personal computers oriented toward educational uses for children, such as Kay's inspirational Dynabook. Doug Engelbart's initiatives invigorated enough disciples that the mouse and multiple windows eventually caught on. PARC pushed forward with a variety of graphic user interfaces including the overlapping windows in Smalltalk, and the tiled strategies in the Xerox STAR. These provided inspiration and ideas for the failed Apple Lisa and then the famed Apple Macintosh.

As an early user of the STAR, I thought the Macintosh interface, which appeared in January 1984, was a big step forward. Larry Tesler added animated dashed rectangles for moving, opening/closing, and resizing of windows. Smooth movements, overlapped windows, consistent pull-down menus, and a mouse-centric interface made the Macintosh much easier to learn and use. Simple pull-down menu operations gave users easy control over text styles, size, and fonts and were a big improvement over the extensive, clumsy property sheets in the STAR. Bill Atkinson's MacPaint program further amplified the feeling of direct manipulation of the objects of interest.

I had coined the term *direct manipulation* in 1981 and filled out the description during 1982, but the major paper "Direct Manipulation: A Step Beyond Programming Languages" appeared in *IEEE Computer* only in August 1983. I had reworked this paper repeatedly based on reviewers' comments, which sharpened the arguments. The central claim was that users would perform best if they could see a visual presentation of the world of action, which included representations of the objects (files, directories, programs) and actions of interest (icon for window closing, printer for printing, trash can for deleting). This was a big step over the command-line interfaces in which users had to memorize commands and type file names to make anything happen. Recognition is far easier for most tasks than recall. Menu selection was a clear step forward but even better were two-dimensional visual presentations that enabled users to select or drag-and-drop objects. Pointing devices could replace the keyboard. Actions could be rapid, incremental, and reversible. Users could drag a file smoothly across the screen and drop it into a folder, or they could simply move it back to where it came from. In graphics programs, users did not have to type a command to place a rectangle on the display; instead, they simply used a "rubber rectangle" which could be resized rapidly, incrementally, and reversibly.

My claims were based on analyses of the "what you see is what you get" (WYSIWYG) word processors that were quickly pushing out the command-line editors with embedded formatting commands. Typing `change /appple/apple/` is more tedious and error prone than placing a cursor next to the p and pressing delete. Additional support for two-dimensional visual presentations came from studying air traffic control systems, video games, the STAR, some simulations, and other advanced systems. The concepts have been validated by experiments, refined for differing contexts, and productively clarified by cognitive psychologists Ed Hutchens, Jim Hollan, and Don Norman (1986). They described how direct manipulation helps users bridge the gulf of execution (the gap between user intention and system capabilities) and the gulf of evaluation (the gap between user expectation and the perceived state of the system).

Direct manipulation ideas faced two challenges. First, designers and researchers had to shift thinking from command-line interfaces and models of human activity that emphasized speed of performance, while downplaying the importance of ease of learning, low error rates, and subjective user satisfaction. These older models, such as the Keystroke-Level Model (KLM) and the Goals, Operators, and Methods, and Selection Rules (GOMS), which had been advocated by Stuart Card, Tom Moran, and Allen Newell in their influential book *The Psychology of Human–Computer Interaction* (1983). I was challenged by an invitation to write a book review for the widely read industry magazine *Datamation* (Shneiderman, 1984). Part of the challenge was that Newell was one of my academic heroes, with whom I sought to go my graduate studies at CMU, until the Viet Nam War draft stopped that plan. While I was eager to celebrate this book that prominently described the emerging field of HCI, my review also pointed to the need to address ease of learning, low error rates, and subjective user satisfaction. Even expert users in the studies reported in their book were making errors about a third of the time. Direct manipulation designs were easy to learn, often prevented errors, and clearly brought high levels of user enthusiasm, which was in stark contrast with the frustration many users found with command-line interfaces. One of my great professional satisfactions was that in his CHI 1985 Conference Keynote Newell highlighted the influence of my 1980 book, *Software Psychology*, on his thinking.

The second challenge to direct manipulation came from those who sought to prove that autonomous machines or agents would be more effective than user driven actions. Some challengers snickered at the idea that users would have to directly manipulate every object, one at a time; they thought that an intelligent agent might recognize the user's intention and carry out a complex task automatically. My 1983 paper anticipated this concern and included a section on direct manipulation programming that would enable users to specify procedures for just such situations when the repetitive tasks would otherwise become too tedious. Notwithstanding some interesting work in end-user programming and programming-by-example, the full notion of direct manipulation programming remains to be widely implemented. The lively discussions of design strategies continued, culminating in debates between me and Pattie Maes of the MIT Media Lab (1997), which are discussed in Section 1.8.

In spite of all the interest in direct manipulation, the growth of the SIGCHI Conferences, and the commercial success of graphical user interfaces, I still had some struggles in my own career, even though the University of Maryland's Human-Computer Interaction Lab, founded in 1983, was seen as an early leader in the field. During the 1980s, I had attracted research funding from companies such as Control Data, IBM, AT&T, Apple, and SUN Microsystems and government agencies such as NASA, National Science Foundation, Department of Interior, Library or Congress, and National Library of Medicine, which enabled me to turn out an ample number of papers.

I taught a popular undergraduate course on Human Factors in Computer and Information Systems starting in 1983, but it was only in 1988 that I was allowed to offer a graduate course on User Interface Design. This finally validated the importance of HCI in my computer science department and gave me better opportunities to attract doctoral students to work with me. While I was successful in writing papers with many undergraduate and graduate students for many years, my first Ph.D. student, Andrew Sears, graduated in 1993, fully 20 years after I got my own Ph.D.

Another indication of the challenges HCI faced in its early days was my struggle to become a Full Professor. I had devoted senior faculty supporters, but some of my more traditional colleagues questioned whether HCI was really part of computer science. These colleagues delayed my request for promotion to full professor from 1987 to 1989. Part of the difficulty was finding respected HCI researchers who were computer science full professors to write reference letters. Several of them have come forward and told me of their good deeds on my behalf, which I always appreciated. I repaid these kindnesses by writing many reference letters for younger colleagues for the past 30 years.

A natural implication of direct manipulation was to shift from keyboards to pointing devices such as the mouse, but we quickly recognized that touchscreens were strong candidates for widespread use. Early applications that we built were for kiosks in museums, homes, and stores, but the attraction of building touchscreen-based mobile devices was irresistible. The low accuracy of existing touchscreens required 1-inch square buttons, so we build a 9-inch wide keyboard for data entry, then shrunk it to 7, 5, and 3 inches. Our studies showed that typing speeds were slower with small screens, but typing was possible if we shifted from the usual selection strategy of "land-on" to selection on "lift-off." Users could put their finger on the screen to get a cursor above their finger, then slide around to place the cursor and activate on lift-off. Our paper at CHI 1988 and other venues told the story, but in some cases reviewers doubted that what we had done was possible, until we submitted a video. The lift-off strategy remains in use for the Apple iPhone and many other mobile devices.

Interest in our touchscreen, home applications, circular pie menus, hypertext, and other prototypes drew a visit from Steve Jobs on Wednesday October 26, 1988. He had come to demonstrate his NeXT computer to educators at the EDUCOM 1988 Conference in Washington, DC. Jobs cruised through our demos quickly declaring "That's Great! That's Great! That Sucks! That's Great! That Sucks!" He had reasons for his reactions, although our studies showed that some of his assumptions were wrong. Still it was a memorable encounter, which contributed to my becoming a consultant and expert witness for Apple.

1.4   PERSONAL COMPUTING TAKES HOLD: MACINTOSH VS. WINDOWS

While advocates of UNIX and command lines defended their territory, the growth of public acceptance of personal computers with graphical user interfaces was astonishing to industry observers. Apple computers had promised a computer "for the rest of us" meaning the non-technically oriented users who wanted to write plays, compose music, or be political organizers. Apple's famous advertisement, which aired during the January 1984 Super Bowl, showed an athletic woman running through a large meeting room with hundreds of drone-like viewers watching the gray image of a Big Brother-like figure. She hurls a sledgehammer to shatter the screen and liberate the drones. Amazing, daring, incredible! Apple's perceived enemy was IBM, but the evil brother for Apple turned out to be Microsoft.

Relations between Apple and Microsoft started out friendly enough, with Bill Gates licensing much of the Apple interface from Steve Jobs in 1985 for a mere $5,000. Gates used this license to bring out Windows 1.0 which had many Apple features such as pull-down menus, icons, and dialog boxes. Detractors labeled these new graphical user interfaces as WIMPs for windows, icons, menus, and pointing devices. This somewhat pejorative term was used by seasoned UNIX users who saw these new easy-to-use interfaces as less potent than their command-line interfaces.

Microsoft's Windows 1.0 used a tiled window strategy that split the screen to accommodate newly opened windows. Unfortunately, the lack of smooth animation, low-resolution screens, and some surprising changes when windows were moved made this version of tiling tricky for users. Gates claimed that his tiling strategy was superior to the messy desktops of overlapping windows, but the marketplace did not buy this argument or the product.

When Windows 2.0 emerged in 1987 employing Apple's overlapping window strategy, Steve Jobs wrote to Gates to complain that this violated the terms of the 1985 license. Gates said he didn't see it that way, so Apple sued for copyright infringement in 1988. I was an expert witness for Apple for five years, until the U.S. Supreme Court refused to hear Apple's appeal in 1993 (Shneiderman, 1993b). My role was to demonstrate that there were many alternatives open to Microsoft and that it did not have to copy Apple's design. Microsoft won because the judge decided to compare interfaces by the visual elements, not by the overall look-and-feel. Since the Macintosh had six one-pixel wide lines in the title bar while Windows had a solid blue field, they were different. The fact that users could only move windows by dragging on the title bar was an invisible feature, so the judge did not consider that similarity important. Since the Macintosh used dotted line animations while Windows used solid thicker lines, they were different. Window resizing and icon dragging animations were also different. Apple lost the case and its chance to hold on to a sizable market.

Still the Apple designers deserve credit for showing that GUIs were technically viable and commercially appealing for non-technical users in education, at home, and in business. They also created a devoted following among graphic designers who loved the visual and direct manipulation style of the interface for their work. Direct manipulation became a key principle in the Apple and Microsoft guidelines, which influenced a generation of designers.

1.5   HYPERTEXT, COMPUTER-SUPPORTED COOPERATIVE WORK, AND MULTIMEDIA ARE BORN

The principles of direct manipulation were widely applied, including improved user interfaces for Bush's 1945 vision, expanded by Ted Nelson's descriptions of hypertext environments. Hypertext became the first of three key movements of the 1980s. The goal of hypertext was to break the tradition of linear text by allowing easy jumps among related topics. Bush applied this idea to following precedents among legal decisions, but jumping to articles about people, places, organizations, or ideas allowed users to get detailed information on demand.

Typical early hypertext designs included paragraphs of text followed by a numbered menu of destinations. A keyboard press of a number initiated a jump to the destination. Some innovators tried to make the design more direct by adding link icons (an anchor in one system and a rectangular card in another) in the paragraph and allow selection by mouse. An even more direct manipulation design was to highlight the appropriate phrase and allow clicking directly on the phrase, which became a key feature of our Hyperties hypertext system, which led to a commercial product from Cognetics Corporation.

Our empirical studies demonstrated the benefits in faster user performance and higher subjective satisfaction for what we called "embedded menus" (Koved and Shneiderman, 1986). A serious test case was the July 1988 issue of the *Communications of the ACM*, which contained seven papers from the first Hypertext Conference held in 1987. We made a Hyperties version (4,000 copies sold) for the IBM PC; a group at Brown University used Apple's HyperCard to make a Macintosh version; and a third group used KMS to make a Sun workstation version. Tim Berners-Lee told me that he adopted the light blue highlighted links in Hyperties, citing our hypertext disk in his Spring 1989 manifesto for the Web. He was clever enough to improve on our academic term "embedded menus" and called the highlighted phrases "hot spots" or "hot links."

The intrigue of hypertext is that it extends traditional linear text with the opportunity for jumping to multiple related articles. For some purposes, hypertext can be a welcome improvement over linear paper documents, but there is a danger that jumping can also lead to hyperchaos. To reduce confusion, hypertext authors needed to choose appropriate projects, to organize their articles suitably, and to adjust their writing style to make the best use of this new medium. The first step in creating effective hypertexts is to choose projects in which

1. there is a large body of information organized into numerous fragments;

2. the fragments relate to one another; and

3. the user needs only a small fraction of the fragments at any time.

The dual dangers are that hypertext may be inappropriate for some projects and that the design of the hypertext may be poor (for example, too many links or a confusing structure). A traditional novel is written linearly, and the reader is expected to read the entire text from beginning to end. Most poems, fairy tales, newspaper articles, and even the chapters of this book are written in a linear form. Of course, hyper-novels, hyper-poems, hyper-fairy tales, hyper-newspapers, and hyper-books emerged, but they required creative rethinking of the traditional forms.

Poor design of hypertext was common: too many links, long chains of links to reach relevant material, or too many long dull articles. Another common problem were the inadequate tables of contents or overviews that made it difficult for users to determine what was contained in the hypertext. Breaking a text into linked fragments did not ensure that the result would be effective, attractive, or useful.

Engelbart's work inspired also a second key movement of the mid-1980s, systems to facilitate collaboration. Researchers who were combining computation and communication held the first conference on Computer-Supported Cooperative Work in 1986, for which I was one of the organizers. High-tech visionaries were promoting high bandwidth connections to support videoconferencing, but the big success story was text-only email and discussion groups. Even slow telephone dial-up connections were adequate for this application and usage soared wherever email became available. This quiet revolution continued as more and more people gain access to email. The surprise was probably most stunning at the companies that were offering "information services" such as stock quotes and airline schedules. These services were being used, but the big generators of connect-minutes and the large income makers were email and discussion groups. Many computing visionaries constantly underestimated users' desire to communicate with others with text-only asynchronous email. They believed video, 3D, and avatars were needed, but simple text-based instant messaging on America Online, discussion groups supported by listservs, and web-based discussions were enormous successes. The new computing was not about what computers could do, it was about what users could do, and users loved being able to send messages to each other.

A third key movement that blossomed in the 1980s was multimedia. In early personal computers the displays often had fewer than 640 × 400 pixels and were monochrome. Photos or videos could be shown on a separate display from a separate device called a videodisc player. As higher-resolution color displays became common and processor speeds increased, it became possible to dispense with the videodisc player and include imagery in applications. Training systems could show animations of how to repair a copier, travel packages could give tours of hotel suites, and educational applications could show videos of lions and tigers and bears. One of the attractions of computer-based multimedia was that users were in control. They could stop, replay, and save animations, tours, or videos.

By the 1990s, the three vibrant technology movements of hypertext, collaboration, and multimedia had drawn active communities of researchers and developers and become part of computing history. They've been amplified, extended, and even superseded by advances such as e-commerce, text messaging, video connections from mobile devices, social media, and augmented/virtual reality.

1.6   THE WORLD WIDE WEB SPREADS

Hyperties and its variations faded as the World Wide Web spread over the planet. Berners-Lee's Web was a brilliant innovation because it made cross-computer links easy. Many of us were appalled with its loosely controlled architecture that did not ensure that links would be updated when changes were made; clearly, we overestimated users' expectations for reliability. The Web and social media provide a remarkable environment for sharing information and working together; they are exemplary media with low entry costs for publishing a magazine, selling new or used goods, and spreading the word about new ideas, products, or political movements.

The Web itself continued to spread during its first decade and raised a new set of user interface concerns. A favorite example is the question of menu hierarchy design. If you have 10,000 items in a product catalog, encyclopedia or event listing, should you have a tree with ten links per level and four levels (10^4), 22 links per level and three levels (22^3), or 100 links per level and two levels (100^2). The argument for ten links per level was that it is faster to scan and simpler to make a choice among ten items than 100 items. The argument for 100 links per level was that fewer decisions are better even if each decision takes a bit longer. Other answers are that it depends on the user or the content of the menu tree. More than a half dozen empirical studies showed consistent speed-ups and increased satisfaction for the broader shallower trees. The effect is strong and dramatic. As long as the menus are well organized, users are more likely to find their information faster with broader shallower trees.

The designers of Yahoo! quickly recognized the broader-shallower principle, leading them to create a web page with more than one hundred links. The *New York Times* web page began with about a dozen links, then grew to about 30 and then 100s. Broader shallower trees give users a clearer overview of what is available and what is not. Broader shallower trees require few steps to get to results while facilitating backtracking and exploration.

However, Google's founders chose to avoid menus and relied on a simple textual entry box so users could type in their queries without distractions. The results, which needed to be browsed, are shown in a scrolling list of choices order by relevance.

But web design is about more than menu hierarchies or search queries for finding destinations, documents, or services. There were so many great research questions about how to combine text and images, how to minimize scrolling while keeping the number of jumps small, and how to accommodate slow and fast network connections. As web page design became fashionable, user interface issues infiltrated airport, cocktail party, and dormitory discussions. Suddenly everyone was ready to critique Disney's or eBay's layout, color choices, and menus.

This was good news because the number of e-commerce sites that were built far exceeded the number of user interface design professionals. Just as word processing users have learned something about layout and fonts that was once in the domain of document designers and graphic artists, website managers acquired some of the skills of user interface designers and experimental researchers.

While narrow questions of user interface design could be studied in hour-long controlled experiments, broader questions of user experience design (UXD) required long-term study of users "in the wild." The shift toward UXD was recognized that designers had to do more than design an interface, they had to design the full user experience that included the branding of products and services, the importance of promoting privacy, safety, trust and loyalty, and the need to focus on long-term experiences as users became proficient.

I later described these complementary directions as micro-HCI and macro-HCI, drawing on the distinctions in micro and macro economics. Micro-HCI covered the small questions of font, color, layout, consistency, menu design, and form fill-in strategies. Micro-HCI questions could be studied with traditional controlled experiments in the laboratory. Macro-HCI covered questions such as how to gain trust for e-commerce, how to assure privacy of personal information, and how to promote safety from cybercriminals. Macro HCI questions had to be studied in the field over weeks or months by observation, interview, survey, or data logging. Social impact issues of macro-HCI quickly emerged, such as protection of children from pornography or stalkers, rights and limits of free speech, frustration from inability to accomplish goals, and dangers of alienation or depression from excessive usage.

Widespread use of the Web produced environments where malicious actors such as criminals, hate groups, and terrorists produced cyber-crime, delivered racially charged threats, and enlisted recruits for violent attacks. These problems and the more recent threats from cyber-attacks, fake news, and election interference, have reduced enthusiasm and usage for social media. Current attempts by leading corporations to limit the problems and governments to regulate activities are still less successful than many commentators would like.

1.7   EIGHT GOLDEN RULES OF USER INTERFACE DESIGN

Lively debates emerged about user interface and experience design issues, putting pressure on me and others to offer a clear and brief set of rules. By 1984 I came up with a set of what I called Eight Golden Rules of User Interface Design (Table 1.1). I taught these in week-long professional development courses at the University of Maryland and UCLA, and then later at the University of California at Santa Cruz. These rules were included in the 1st edition of *Designing the User Interface* (1987).

Table 1.1: Eight Golden Rules of User Interface Design
1.   Strive for consistency.
2.   Enable frequent users to use shortcuts.
3.   Offer informative feedback.
4.   Design dialogs to yield closure.
5.   Offer error prevention and simple error handling.
6.   Permit easy reversal of actions.
7.   Support internal locus of control.
8.   Reduce short-term memory load.

A promising young researcher, Jakob Nielsen, attended my public course and then extended the list to ten rules. He did strong research at Sun Microsystems and then went on to form the Norman Nielsen Group with Don Norman in 1993. Their successful partnership and widely read books helped spread user interface design in business, earning Nielsen the title of "guru of web design?"

I was amused to see how widely these ideas were picked up, including in YouTube video parodies. I've kept to my eight rules, but they have evolved over time, so in the 6th edition (2016) the rules are now (changes in bold face) (Table 1.2).

Table 1.2: Revised Eight Golden Rules of User Interface Design (changes in bold face)
1. Strive for consistency.
2. **Seek universal usability**.
3. Offer informative feedback.
4. Design dialogs to yield closure.
5. **Prevent errors**.
6. Permit easy reversal of actions.
7. **Keep users in control**.
8. Reduce short-term memory load.

The shift to universal usability was meant to strength attention to diverse users, especially users with disabilities. I coined this term to suggest stronger goals than merely accessible interfaces. Universal usability was motivated by increasing recognition that designing for diverse users typically helps improve the user experience for all users. Inspirational examples were that sidewalk curb cuts and closed captioning, both designed for users with disabilities, had benefits to many users. Similarly, audio interfaces, larger buttons, and font size controls have brought benefits to many users.

1.8   DIRECT MANIPULATION VS. INTELLIGENT AGENTS

A more acrimonious and continuing debate emerged over the questions of direct manipulation vs. anthropomorphic or agent-based designs. Panels that I participated in at the Computer Human Interaction (CHI) annual conference produced lively encounters in 1992, 1995, and 1996. The early panel focused on the use of human-like characters in user interfaces. Advocates, influenced by AI mimicry scenarios, felt that such characters would be comforting to novices and encourage their use of computers. Although early bank machines had tried this (Tillie the Teller, Harvey Wallbanker, and Johnny Cash), they failed just as badly as talking cars and soda machines. It seemed to me that users wanted control over their tools, rather than a relationship with them. Control became central.

In the second of the panels, promoters of Microsoft BOB retreated from the arguments about human forms and claimed that cartoon-like characters would be more acceptable so as not to suggest that the computer could do everything that a human could. They still felt that "social interfaces" were the key to user acceptance and emphasized adaptive behavior to accommodate changing patterns of interaction. This argument violated my growing belief in the importance of user control and need for predictable interfaces. Users seemed to want the dependability and safety of a predictable interface: they wanted to be able to go through the same patterns and see familiar system responses, or show an interface to a colleague and be assured that the colleague could reproduce the same results.

In fact, I had a neat empirical demonstration from a student project that was designed to change my mind and show me the benefits of adaptive systems. Chris Mitchell designed a Chinese restaurant ordering system that moved more frequently ordered items, such as wonton soup, closer to the top of the menu to speed selection. His experiment backfired, since speed and preference favored the stable menus. The disruption of changing menu positions had undermined the benefits of fast selection for frequent items. Predictable behavior won out.

As for Microsoft BOB, after its highly publicized release in March 1995, its cartoon dog character Rover and friends were discontinued in early 1996. My outspoken opposition and public encounters with Cliff Nass of Stanford University elicited a phone call from Melinda Gates (Bill Gates's wife), who was the marketing manager for BOB, asking me why I was so opposed to these social interfaces. I expected that Microsoft would somehow keep promoting BOB and develop version 2.0, but it was absolutely gone in a year.

After the third CHI conference panel, I was invited to a more confrontational debate format with Pattie Maes, at the ACM Intelligent User Interfaces conference (Shneiderman and Maes, 1997). Maes was a media dream: an accomplished MIT professor who was featured in *People Magazine* as among the fifty most beautiful people in the world. Pundits and even my friends were quick to label this debate as Beauty vs. the Beast (Figure 1.6). She was not advocating anthropomorphic designs, but rather invisible agents that would carry out your wishes by recognizing patterns of behavior or making good guesses about your needs. Agents would recommend movies, steer you to important email, and find you cheap airline tickets.

Figure 1.6: Opening spread for article on the debate from *ACM Interactions* (Nov/Dec 1997).

Who wouldn't want such services, if they were effective. But the grand promises based on vague specifications or natural language input seemed hard to realize and my belief strengthened in comprehensible, predictable, and controllable interfaces. The agents concept may be appealing to some, but when reality sets in and design decisions have to be made, direct manipulation seemed to be the preferred path. Maes's company, which began as Agents, Inc., was renamed Firefly and the interface was simply drop-down menus. Its film recommending system was an intriguing application of her group process ideas by which users specify which films they liked and disliked and got recommendations for films based on matches with other users. Firefly was bought by Microsoft and recommender systems have emerged nicely in e-commerce environments such as Netflix and Amazon, which made suggestions for movies and books based on buying patterns of other users.

I argued that ambitious agents whose behavior was hard to follow undermined the users' satisfaction in accomplishing their work. Users want to believe that they did a good job, not that some intelligent agent did it for them. Similarly, users need to be responsible for mistakes and failures, so they need to be able to monitor and understand what they are doing. If an agent or expert system produces unpredictable results, then users will feel out of control and not responsible. This unacceptable position leads most users to prefer direct manipulation strategies that are comprehensible because they are consistent, predictable, and controllable. I was delighted to see that several months after our debate, Pattie Maes was promoting user responsibility as a key aspect of design; unfortunately, the community of researchers surrounding the Autonomous Agents conference rejected the suggestion to include topics such as "monitoring agents" or "visualization of agent behavior."

Twenty years after the 1997 debate, Pattie Maes and I were brought back together at the CHI 2017 conference to reflect on what had changed. We both spoke warmly and respectfully about each other's contributions. Pattie Maes had helped organize the annual ACM Augmented Human conference, which built on the terminology from Doug Engelbart. I had to acknowledge the obvious success of recommender systems, envisioned by Maes and brought to fruition by the work of Joseph Konstan, John Riedl, Paul Resnick, and others, and speech-based personal assistant technologies such as Siri, Alexa, Cortana, etc. These are valuable additions for some user tasks, but I still believe that supporting user control by visual methods and touchscreen mobile devices will remain the dominant interaction forms.

While debates about user control vs. autonomous agents continue, a related issue is the continuing discussion of humanoid robots. These have long been a dream for some designers, with bold ideas such as Ananova the news reader, Honda's near-life-size Asimo, and recently Hanson Robotics Sophia, who was granted Saudi Arabian citizenship. While these capture the attention of journalists, commercial success comes to designers who offer comprehensible, predictable, and controllable interfaces which enable users to get what they need done, such as checking out of supermarkets, checking in at airports, or checking up on their sleeping babies.

1.9   VISUALIZATION

The direct manipulation ideas and implementations naturally led our HCIL research group to consider more intense use of visualization to present information in compact formats that facilitated exploration. As far back as 1991 we were already working on two major ideas: dynamic queries for interactive exploration and treemaps to show large amounts of hierarchical data.

The dynamic queries ideas were applied for an interactive version of the Periodic Table of Elements and the bold HomeFinder (finding a home in a real estate database of the Washington, DC area) encouraged us further, while bringing widespread interest by way of our CHI 1992 videos and paper. IBM wanted an innovative interface to explore a database of 10,000 videos, pushing us to produce a 2D zoomable prototype, called the FilmFinder. Christopher Ahlberg put his interest in films, especially those with the attractive Michelle Pfeiffer, to work implementing the FilmFinder, which became our most widely circulated demo and influential CHI 1994 paper. Then he formed a company in 1997 to develop the Spotfire commercial tool. I served on the board of directors for five years as Ahlberg grew the company to 200 people, leading to its sale in 2007. Spotfire remains a leading commercial information visualization tool. The dynamic queries interactive visual approach drew the interest of Richard Saul Wurman, the founder of the TED conferences, who invited me to speak at the 1998 TED (Technology Entertainment and Design) Conference in Monterey, CA. It was a remarkable experience to be with 2000 industry leaders and to be included in the extraordinary set of speakers that included architect Frank Gehry, Oracle's Larry Ellison, evangelist Billy Graham, and Lion King creator Julie Taymor.

The second key visualization idea was treemaps, which were motivated by my desire to produce a single screen display that showed the contents of an entire hard drive, with its many levels of folders and files. I struggled for months to find a visual design that showed every folder and file on the screen at once, with each folder represented by a rectangle that was proportional to its file size. Then one day in the campus faculty lounge I had the Aha! moment when I figured out how to do it. It took several days to write the six lines of recursive code to implement the algorithm, and then Brian Johnson built working systems for his Ph.D. dissertation. Our early designs took a bit of work to understand, but the benefits were clear to us. I spoke about the idea of treemaps at the University of Washington in January 1993 generating skeptical responses from my audience. But when we went to their lab, inserted the disk and reviewed the contents of the hard drive there were clear gasps of discovery. The treemap display revealed that a large part of their hard drive was filled with three unnecessary copies of a big compiler program. The demo worked, but many improvements to treemaps were needed to make is successful for stock market, health, economic, and many other forms of data (Shneiderman et al., 2011). Treemaps became widely used in applications and on websites, then integrated in Microsoft's Excel and most commercial information visualization products.

Later work on information visualization led to the NodeXL package for social network analysis and visualization, which has become the most widely used tool for education. Another decade-long effort was on our family of event sequence visualization tools that were put to work for understanding patterns of treatment outcomes from electronic health record systems.

I continue to believe that researchers and analysts in every field can use interactive information visualization tools for:

- more effective detection of faulty data, missing data, unusual distributions, and anomalies;

- deeper and more thorough data analyses that produce profounder insights; and

- richer understandings that enable researchers to ask bolder questions.

CHAPTER 2

The Growth of HCI and User Interface/Experience Design: Presented as a Tire-Tracks Diagram

2.1 INTRODUCTION

My 3-year old grandson Milo deftly swipes his mother's iPhone to look at photos, confidently scanning forward and backward. Milo quickly learned how to navigate hierarchies, assumes that words and images are clickable, and plays music when he wants to. In just a few decades, the astonishing growth of interactive systems has transformed the world, enabling people to connect with family and friends, get medical advice, conduct business, or organize political movements. The remarkably rapid dissemination of HCI research has brought profound changes that enrich people's lives, while also producing a new set of problems, such as user frustration, inequality of access, and threats from malicious actors.

Early studies built on traditional controlled experimental human factors studies, but creative HCI researchers quickly adopted new research methods that combined quantitative and qualitative methods, while applying narrowly focused hypothesis testing with broader case study methods. The early experimental results from the 1970s were distilled into the guidelines described in "Human Factors Experiments in Designing Interactive Systems" (Shneiderman, 1979), which were then further refined during the 1980s into extensive guidelines documents from Apple, Microsoft, and other organizations. These guidelines documents and their progeny became international standards, which shaped the products that are embedded in office, mobile, entertainment, and educational applications [Shneiderman, 2017].

This chapter describes processes by which HCI has become a widely successful research discipline pursuing new ideas and theories, while User interface/eXperience Design (UXD) has become an influential profession supporting business needs. UX designers seek to win over new users and retain them for the long-term, for reduce frustration and promote user satisfaction, and to ensure privacy and security. Simple charts and a tire-tracks diagram presents visual evidence of disciplinary growth.

Within the HCI and UXD communities there is a great sense of pride in what has been accomplished during the 36 years since the historically significant 1982 Gaithersburg conference on "Human Factors in Computing Systems," which many see as the starting point for these topics. There were a few workshops earlier, but this conference drew a surprising crowd of 906 attendees, signaling strong interest in the topic and helping launch the ACM's SIGCHI (Shneiderman, 1986). The conference series was then taken over by SIGCHI, which has grown to be a large professional group, which in addition to its main annual conference, sponsors 35 smaller conferences on specialized topics. HCI research has also become an international activity with professional societies, academic programs, and industrial impact worldwide.

The trajectory of this research began with carefully controlled studies of individual users carrying out key tasks requiring perceptual, cognitive, and motor skills. I was an early enthusiast of these methods, since they represented rigorous scientific research, but I realized that new methods were needed. The growth of interest in communication tasks required study of pairs and groups of users, which expanded to research on online communities; in turn, these online communities evolved into social media experiences for billions of users. The older reductionist models of research, which remain valid and useful, might be characterized as micro-HCI, which focuses on narrowly defined tasks that can be studied in one to three hours. By contrast, macro-HCI focuses on richer aspects of user experiences, such as relationship-building, empathy, and trust, which require study over weeks and months. Admirably a growing number of HCI researchers see their scope as including economic development, community safety, peace studies, environmental sustainability, and energy conservation (Shneiderman et al., 2016b).

2.2   EXPLOSIVE GROWTH IN HCI PUBLICATIONS

Thoughtful reviews of HCI's history were written by Myers (1998) and Grudin (2016). Also careful bibliometric and scientometric analyses were undertaken by Barkhuus and Rode (2007), Bartneck and Hu (2009), and Henry et al. (2007). These are valuable for their insights, but I was eager to consider measures of growth that might indicate broader impact.

A natural way to begin documenting the growth of a discipline is to look at the published papers. Fortunately, the heroic efforts of Gary Perlman give a clear picture of the dramatic growth of papers in conferences and journals (Figure 2.1). His HCI Bibliography website (www.hcibib.org) constitutes a definition of what is in the discipline and what is not. His definition of the scope of HCI have been tested by time, through challenges by journal editors, questions by conference journal editors, and feedback from users. The data show remarkable growth from only 74 entries (papers in conferences and journals) published in 1980 to an astounding 11,165 entries in 2014. This 150-fold growth shows the vibrant activity in an unquestionable way. By 2018, there were approximately 30 journals and 120 yearly conferences focusing on HCI research, while many other conferences and journals regularly publish special issues, sections, or individual papers on HCI research.

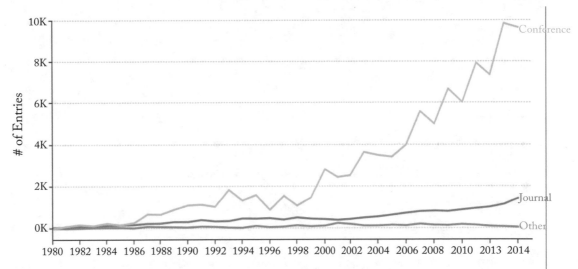

Figure 2.1: Growth in the HCI Bibliography abstracts from 74–11,165 entries during 1980–2014, mainly from conference and journal papers (http://www.hcibib.org/pubdates.html).

Another way to track the growth of a discipline is through the use of the free publicly accessible Google Ngram Viewer that covers almost 20 million English-language book. This web-based tool allows users to submit words and phrases and get a graph that shows the frequency of those words over time, as a percent of all words in the dataset. A simple search on "usability, user interface, user experience, human-computer interaction," shows the dramatic growth since 1982 (Figure 2.2). User interface and usability have grown substantially, while user experience and HCI are less frequent in this broad collection of books. Since books are written for wider audiences than research articles, it is natural that user interface and usability are much more frequently used than HCI. Similarly, the promoters of user experience as a newer term in the past two decades have yet to produce the impact they wish in published books.

A third way to assess the growth of HCI is through a mainstream news source such as the *New York Times*. Their frequency of mentions shows growth in documents that refer to the component terms (Figure 2.3). While not as dramatic as the other sources, it still shows substantial increase.

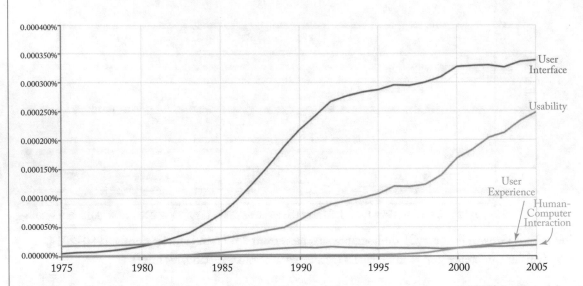

Figure 2.2: Growth in usage of terms (user interface, usability, user experience, and HCI) in Google's Ngram Viewer https://books.google.com/ngrams.

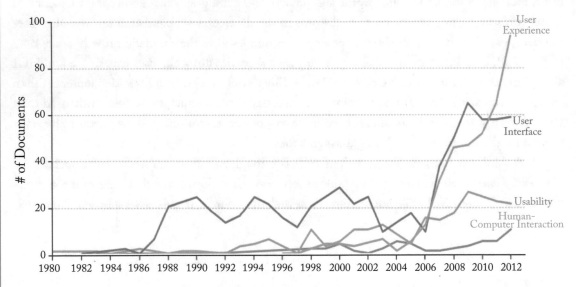

Figure 2.3: Growth in usage of terms (user interface, usability, user experience, and HCI) in *The New York Times* from 1980–2012. Information provided from internal *New York Times* resources. The data for the past few years was incomplete and was removed.

2.3   TIRE-TRACKS DIAGRAM FOR HCI

A tire-tracks diagram provides a useful overview of HCI achievements. For more than two decades, such diagrams have been eagerly shown by policy-oriented information technology advocates in Washington, DC to Congressional staffers, funding agency directors, business leaders, journalists, and anyone who would look (NRC, 1995, 2003, 2012). Twice I joined colleagues to walk the lobbies of the U.S. House and Senate buildings to meetings with the Representatives, Senators, and staffers who had agreed to meet with us. We trained about guided by the Computing Research Association staff, who provided folders with tire-tracks diagrams to explain the importance of federal support for university research. These diagrams show tracks for university projects, industry research and development, and products that grow into $1B and $10B markets. Arrows criss-cross the tracks showing the vital connections between these three tracks, such as a Ph.D. student going to work in industry, a research paper leading to new products, or an industry visit to an academic research lab.

Sets of these tracks for Personal Computing, Internet and Web, Enterprise Systems, and other market segments give the impression of tire tracks. The designers' goal was to show that federal funding of early-stage university projects, which are closely linked with industry research, is the catalyst for much of the subsequent commercial success of information technologies. The tire-tracks diagrams proved to be a convincing way of showing the impact of federal funding and the efficacy of academic-industry connections in propelling new technologies to market success. Of course, this is a simplified model of reality in which there are troubling setbacks, returns to earlier issues, and entangled themes. The developers of the early tire-tracks diagram were making trying to tell a simple story of progress, so turbulent realities and incomplete evidence were cleansed from the diagram.

The developers of the 1995 tire-tracks diagrams told me about their personal recollections of technology transfer by students who went to work in industry, industrial researchers visiting academic centers, and key papers that influenced product development. Their informal approach, with links added where they thought appropriate, was turned into a simplified diagram that made a strong impression on those who studied it. The Computing Research Associations regularly uses these tire-tracks diagrams in its U.S.-based lobbying effort.

I followed this approach and expanded on Brad Myers' tire-tracks diagram for the HCI field (1998) that emphasized concepts such as direct manipulation, the mouse, and hypertext. My expanded tire-tracks diagram (Figure 2.4) considers progress in seven main areas.

1. Our lab's **hypertext** research led to a 1987 commercial version of highlighted selectable links (www.cs.umd.edu/hcil/hyperties). Tim Berners-Lee used that work as a guide to the light-blue clickable hot spots, which helped the World Wide Web to succeed. Similarly, faceted menus and other interface features facilitated the growth of e-commerce into a booming industry. Increased access to information, expanded

communications services, global collaboration, enhanced creative capacity, and new business models (e.g., eBay, Etsy, Airbnb, Uber, Lyft) continue to transform the world.

2. **Direct manipulation** theories were put to work in touchscreen applications that increased the appeal of mobile devices. Graphical user interfaces enable users to see objects of interest, then make gestures (e.g., click, swipe, drag, pinch) to do what they want. Visual displays with selectable objects reduce learning and speed performance.

3. Early **bulletin boards** matured into blogs, wikis, and reviews that deliver volumes of user-provided content that far exceeded expectations. These laid the foundation for widely used recommender systems, and social networking.

4. The complex interfaces in early **database and information retrieval** languages were replaced by easy-to-use search user interfaces and spoken queries, which produced hugely successful companies such as Google and Baidu.

5. The same story of exponential growth happened as early **teleconferencing** systems expanded into chat, texting, video conferencing, and social media, now delivered by massive companies such as Facebook, Twitter, WhatsApp, and Weibo.

6. **Multimedia** ideas were naturally connected to computing, so it was inevitable that music and photos would become part of the personal computer revolution. As the web's capacity to deliver videos improved, the interest in downloading Hollywood films became widespread, but only a few of the visionaries foresaw that uploading videos would become such an amazing success story. Virtual and augmented reality are poised to become the next phase of what used to be called multimedia.

7. Simple **videogames** paved the way for a vibrant industry that created a gamer culture with both positive and negative impacts. In parallel, simple educational simulations became rich educational platforms, such as Massively Open Online Courses (MOOCs), engaging inquiry-based learning environments, and compelling creativity support tools.

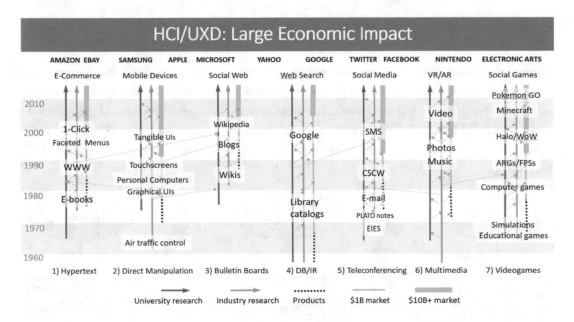

Figure 2.4: The path to success for HCI and User interface/Experience Design is shown in the movement of research from universities to industry. This movement yields products with huge markets.

My goal was to highlight the ways early research at universities and industry laid the foundation for $1B and later $10B markets. Since no one has recorded the careers for every doctoral student, visits between researchers and developers, or all readers of papers, we can never have the full story. Although the accuracy of each mark on the tire-tracks diagram can legitimately be questioned as can what is omitted, the overall story conveys a useful message about how research can lead to markets and how close contacts with markets can increase the impact of basic research. As more evidence is collected, future tire-tracks diagrams will show more complete and accurate evidence of the positive feedback between markets and research.

The tire-tracks diagram focuses on commercial outcomes, but there are many activities within an emerging discipline that influence these outcomes. Key activities are conferences, journals, degree programs, and funding programs. Furthermore, there are necessary changes to an emerging discipline as research methods evolve, as professional societies form, and as curricula shift to include new methods and theories. A separate diagram could focus on the evolution of research methods, principles, guidelines, and theories. The choice of which research topics and markets to include is a subjective process that is meant to provide a description of how ideas travel and businesses grow. Adding information about unproductive research and failed products would be helpful to students and future entrepreneurs. The lessons from failures can be as instructive as those from successes.

2.4   THREE-STAGE PROCESS FROM EXPERIMENTS TO USER SUCCESS

Guideline documents are central to the potent three-stage process that transforms experimental results into user benefits (Figure 2.5). Consider a simplified model of this three-stage process: (1) experimental results from a few thousand researchers were packaged into practical guidelines documents, which (2) influenced the design of widely used software tools that enabled a few million developers to produce mobile, desktop, and web applications, which in turn (3) were used by a few billion people.

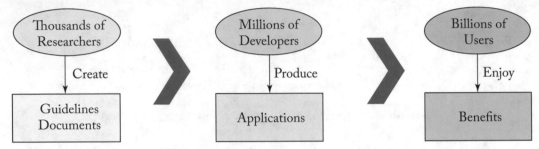

Figure 2.5: The three-stage process by which HCI research and resulting guidelines have broad impact.

This three-stage process meant that the experimental results about consistency, error prevention, direct manipulation, user control, and other golden rules (Section 1.7) propagated outward at warp speed, accelerating the work of developers whose products brought benefits to users around the world. While early guidelines focused on the user interface features, e.g., "ensure visual consistency" or user familiar fonts," later guidelines emphasized user experience issues, e.g., "clarify security and privacy" or "design for customer loyalty."

Of course, other factors contributed to the success of HCI. Sometimes an inspirational prototype triggered new ways of thinking that were followed by product developers. Other times successful commercial products had innovative user interface widgets that triggered many variations and novel explorations. Industrial development methods such as usability testing had an enormous impact in generating data to speed design improvements. Vigorous debates about how to do usability testing, especially how many subjects were needed, accelerated adoption and refinement.

2.5   PROFESSIONAL OBLIGATIONS

Although the creativity and productivity facilitated by rapid progress in interface design are astounding, any widely used technology also generates problems when malicious actors put them to work for criminal, terrorist, and oppressive purposes. Researchers, developers, and distributors of user interfaces have a professional obligation to work with positive forces that best serve human needs, promote fairness, and support dignity. These principles of user experience design have become increasingly important.

One way that HCI researchers serve positive goals and promote widespread dissemination is by seeking universal usability. From the early days, HCI researchers sought to address the needs of all users: young and old, novice and expert, women and men, as well as users with disabilities. By attending to the needs of diverse users, they designed user experiences that were better for all. HCI researchers can be especially proud that the Web Content Accessibility Guidelines (https://www.w3.org/TR/WCAG21/) have improved the accessibility of the World Wide Web across the globe.

As challenges emerge from cyber-criminals, fake news promoters, violent terrorists, and oppressive governments, HCI researchers must improve existing strategies for building trust, encouraging productive deliberation, and resolving conflicts.

2.6 CONCLUSION

In summary, the HCI research community has grown from producing under 100 papers per year in the 1970s to more than 15,000 papers a year. Innovative designs continue to trigger new experiments, which lead to refined guidelines; repeating the three-stage process that brings commercial successes. As long as HCI researchers and designers continue to develop new user interfaces and experiences, there will be a need for fresh experiments and improved guidelines.

Tracking the trajectory of disciplinary success and understanding the underlying components is a difficult job, but one that is worthwhile to understand how different fields grow or dissipate. Chapter 3 is an attempt to record the many components of disciplinary birth. Improved quantitative data would help validate trends, as would a clearer theory of what drives success or failure. A truly valuable theory would assess the role of individuals, universities, industry, and professional societies, as well as the alignment with broader societal movements that are tied to the discipline.

CHAPTER 3

Starting a Discipline and Launching an Industry

3.1 INTRODUCTION

There is a lot more to starting a discipline than writing a few papers or teaching a novel seminar course. The many components of success documented in this chapter may have lessons for others who seek to establish new disciplines or promote new directions in older ones.

As I studied the components of nascent disciplines, it seemed that founders were often motivated by new problems and invigorated by new research methods. This process might be called "paradigm birth" rather than Thomas Kuhn's "paradigm shift," as described in his *Structure of Scientific Revolutions* (1962). Kuhn's paradigm shifts occur when normal science theories can no longer explain observed data, but paradigms are born when new problems and opportunities enable fresh theories and experiments to produce useful knowledge, where no discipline existed before.

This chapter describes processes by which the paradigm births of HCI and UXD gave us happy fraternal twins: a remarkably successful research discipline and an amazingly influential profession. HCI and UXD have hugely affected the lives of almost all people alive today; so, I hope these processes for paradigm birth can be harnessed to create other disciplines and industries that have equal or greater benefits.

HCI's paradigm birth came from the happy union of computing technologies with psychological research methods. The early research and design efforts focused on airplane cockpits and industrial control rooms, while later work was associated with the rapidly growing domain of programming languages and then user interfaces (Shneiderman, 1980). As HCI and UXD grew, their devotion to universal usability promoted widespread successes in e-commerce, productivity tools, online education, multimedia, and social media.

This chapter highlights only a small number of the many HCI/UXD contributions that were needed. There are thoughtful and more thorough historical reviews of HCI (Grudin, 2016; Myers, 1998) and excellent citation analyses (Barkhuus and Rode, 2007; Bartneck and Hu, 2009; Guha et al., 2013; Henry et al., 2007). This chapter was written as a guide for those who are starting fresh disciplines and launching new industries (Grodal et al., 2015) based on the evolution of HCI/UXD. The National Research Council reports (1995, 2003, 2012), which include the tire-tracks diagram to show the evolution from information technology research to products, provide a foundation for this personal reflection. Chapter 2 shows the cross-fertilization between academic research and industry research, which has facilitated billion dollar markets where none existed before (Shneiderman, 2017).

3.2   COMPONENTS OF SUCCESS

Young scholars working in an established discipline assume that their community has always been around; in contrast for older scholars, struggle for acceptance was a key feature of their career trajectory. Young scholars doing HCI research often show admirable self-confidence as they present papers in conferences and publish papers in journals that are older than they are. However, those who were the conference initiators and journal founding editors have worked hard to establish the field, define its research methods, launch degree programs, and develop funding sources from government agencies and companies.

Similarly, young professionals in HCI/UXD self-confidently launch startups, while senior professionals look on in astonishment at their billion-dollar payouts. The growth of HCI and UXD is filled with compelling stories of visionary thinkers, passionate researchers, and inspired entrepreneurs. It has the drama of young scholars challenging conventional thinking, bold innovators competing for billion-dollar markets, and fervent dreamers who sought to change the world—some succeeded and became cultural icons.

Several components seem to have been essential to this successful paradigm birth (Figure 3.1). These components emerged in different orders at universities, businesses, publishers, funding agencies, and professional societies, but I loosely group them into the early components and then the later components.

- **Controlled experiments, qualitative methods, usability testing:** Early HCI research grew out of psychological controlled experiments on perceptual, motor, and cognitive tasks that could be carried out in a laboratory setting within a few hours. These micro-HCI studies remain important, but macro-HCI studies that emphasize ethnographic observation and qualitative methods over months grew in importance for studying trust formation, empathy growth, and community development. UXD practitioners quickly developed usability testing strategies, A/B testing strategies, and web-based logging of actual usage patterns to resolve design decisions.

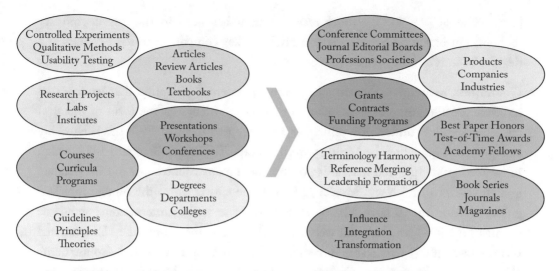

Figure 3.1: The early and later components of successful paradigm birth in the case of HCI and UXD.

- **Research projects, labs, institutes:** HCI was also born out of human factors studies, which early leaders such as Brian Shackel (1962) built on at Loughborough University when he formed the HUSAT (Human Sciences and Advanced Technology) Research Institute. These and other researchers sought to understand how computer displays, input devices, and command languages could be designed to enable users of air traffic control, military, and medical systems to be more effective by speeding performance, lowering error rates, and shortening learning time (Edmonds and Lee, 1974). Visionary leaders, such as J.C.R. Licklider coined the phrase "man-computer symbiosis" (1960). These projects soon expanded into labs inside corporations (e.g., Xerox PARC), or government-funded research labs (e.g., SRI) and then larger institutes at universities, such as our Human-Computer Interaction Lab (HCIL) at the University of Maryland in 1983, the Cognitive Science and Machine Intelligence Lab at the University of Michigan in 1985, and the Media Lab at MIT in 1985.

- **Courses, curricula, programs:** Another component of success is the development of a course on the new discipline, typically housed in a related discipline. Starting in 1991, Terry Winograd's influential, and long-standing seminar at Stanford University's Computer Science Department was titled "People, Computers, and Design" (https://hci.stanford.edu/courses/cs547/abstracts/93-94/940304-winograd.html). While early HCI courses were often given in computer science or psychology departments, there were also courses in industrial engineering, business, education, and library schools

(Hewett et al., 1992). The more recent growth has been in the interdisciplinary iSchools (Information Schools) where HCI is a key component in their courses and degrees (Churchill, Bowser, and Preece, 2013).

- **Guidelines, principles, theories:** Key components of a discipline that launches an industry are the compact encapsulation of new knowledge in the form of practical guidelines, widely understood principles, and accepted theories. HCI has been richly engaged with guidelines beginning with the early US Military Standard 1472, which influenced guidelines and standards documents in many countries, as did the detailed guidelines from Smith and Mosier (1986). These efforts led to the human interface guidelines documents from Microsoft and Apple as well as international standards such as ISO 9241 and national web standards such as those from the U.S. National Cancer Institute. A remarkable success story was the World Wide Web Consortium's Web Content Accessibility Guidelines, which have been adopted in almost every nation that promotes web accessibility. The battles over design principles and theories enriched HCI by demonstrating that there were powerful cognitive, motor, and perceptual factors at work (Rogers, 2012). Later work emphasized the role of social theories of social media and mobile devices.

- **Articles, review articles, books, textbooks:** Soon enough, the growth of articles from less than 100/year to more than 15,000/year demonstrated the explosive growth of HCI. These included influential review articles, which organized an emerging topic, highlighted the influential papers, and anointed the significant researchers. Then came the narrowly focused research books that identified subfields (Shneiderman, 1980; Card et al., 1983), the authoritative edited books (Norman and Draper, 1986), and eventually the widely used textbooks that serve newcomers (Shneiderman, 1987). My book, *Designing the User Interface*, was enhanced by Catherine Plaisant joining as a co-author starting with the 4th edition. The 6th edition, which had other co-authors, appeared in 2016. At the British Open University, Jennifer Preece (chair), Yvonne Rogers, and Laurie Keller developed the first large-scale distance-learning course on HCI in 1990, collaboratively with the Dutch Open University, leading to a widely used book in 1994. Helen Sharp, Yvonne Rogers, and Jennifer Preece produced a widely used textbook, *Interaction Design*, which is in its 5th edition (2019). Don Norman's book on *The Design of Everyday Things*, a hugely successful trade book for general readers, popularized the ideas and processes of usability. It was originally published in 1988 as *The Psychology of Everyday Things*, but was then retitled and eventually republished in a revised edition (Norman, 2013).

- **Presentations, workshops, conferences:** The success of research projects was propagated by early leaders visiting colleagues to give presentations of their work, leading to small workshops, seminars, tutorials, and discussion groups. Once these small events generated enough interest, the key participants sought to create larger conferences as was done in Ann Arbor, MI in May 1981 (Raben et al., 1981), Gaithersburg, MD in March 1982 (Nichols and Schneider, 1982; Shneiderman, 1986), and Manchester, UK in July 1982 (IEE, 1982). Many more conferences followed, weaving together a network of researchers with shared interests. I began doing week-long short courses, mostly for professionals, at the University of Maryland almost every year starting 1980, then added courses at UCLA in 1984, and at University of California-Santa Cruz starting in 1987. These were memorable events, but traveling so much was difficult, so in 1988 I shifted to doing an annual satellite TV course originating from the University of Maryland, starting in October 1988 and going until 1997 (http://www.cs.umd.edu/projects/uis/). These broadcasts were shown at up to 150 sites each year reaching thousands of professionals. Each five-hour broadcast included guest lectures by other HCI Pioneers, such as Don Norman, Jim Foley, Judy Olson, Jakob Nielsen, Jack Carroll, Brenda Laurel, Marilyn Mantei, Aaron Marcus, Joy Mountford, Brad Myers, and Andries van Dam.

- **Degrees, departments, colleges:** Once courses are established and student interest demonstrated, the courses are often shaped into certificate, minor, or full degree programs. Later departments and colleges address the emerging discipline. Within HCI, the creation of the School of Information at the University of Michigan (1996) marked an administrative change that stabilized the position of HCI and related topics, creating a school devoted "to prepare socially engaged information professionals, and to create people-centered knowledge, systems and institutions for the Information Age." Other influential examples of administrative commitments to HCI were the establishment of Georgia Tech's Graphics, Visualization and Usability Lab in 1991 (http://www.gvu.gatech.edu/) and Carnegie Mellon University's Human-Computer Interaction Institute in 1993 (https://www.hcii.cmu.edu/). Our University of Maryland Human-Computer Interaction Lab (http://hcil.umd.edu), formed in 1983, has also been successful, but we remain a more informal association of faculty with shared interests (Shneiderman et al., 2013).

- **Conference committees, journal editorial boards, professional societies:** The lists of conference committees and journal editorial boards demonstrate that a new discipline is coalescing around a network of people who are ready to put their efforts behind it. A set of respected names from respected institutions builds trust for younger researchers, indicating that they are safe to submit their research to these venues. Eventually, groups within existing professional societies support the new discipline, but bolder approaches, such as starting a new professional society, may accelerate progress. Within HCI, the ACM SIGCHI quickly gained recognition in the U.S., eventually sponsoring a large annual conference and 35+ smaller conferences. Similar groups formed in the United Kingdom, France, Germany, Italy, Scandinavia, Australia, and elsewhere, while international organizations such as the International Federation for Information Processing (IFIP) sponsored their own conferences, such as the INTERACT series. Practitioner-oriented groups such as the Usability Professionals Association (UPA) formed in 1994, and later became the User Experience Professionals Association (https://uxpa.org/).

- **Grants, contracts, funding programs:** Early research funding for HCI came from companies that were competing to make better bank machines, consumer devices, educational technology, and healthcare systems; slowly, government funding became available. Often, mission-oriented agencies like NASA, Census, Defense, and the Library of Congress gave grants or contracts to carry out advanced work that drove practical applications and theory development. The UK Science and Engineering Research Council organized the Roberts panel, which in 1982 led to increased funding, as did the Alvey Project; both strongly emphasized "man-computer interaction." Eventually, HCI was supported by National Science Foundation programs and now is included in a growing number of NSF divisions and in programs at many other agencies. HCI has become part of many branches of information and computing technologies such as cybersecurity, data science, information visualization, virtual/augmented reality, mobile devices, and social media. These affiliations may lead to funding from university-industry-government partnerships such as the successful U.S.-based advanced manufacturing initiatives or UK-based Innovate UK. Contemporary shifts to seek the twin-win of research papers and disseminated solutions is already working out favorably for HCI researchers (Shneiderman, 2016).

- **Terminology harmony, reference merging, leadership formation:** Substantial work is necessary to bring the divergent threads of a new discipline into harmony. The effort consists of resolving differences in terminology (e.g., shifting from user interface design to user experience design), which clarifies the key concepts and enables more successful collaborations. Another sign of maturation for a discipline is the process of identifying the key references that define the field. These steps typically promote some researchers to leadership positions, such as editing journals, organizing conferences, and giving keynote addresses.

- **Influence, integration, transformation:** In addition to HCI focused disciplines, HCI has steadily increased its influence in diverse disciplines, such as parts of courses in engineering, business, education, library science, and beyond. Eventually, whole courses and major commitments to HCI have grown in these disciplines, transforming them to be variations on HCI, while related initiatives are invigorating digital humanities and media studies. In some cases, HCI has moved out of computer science departments, but in many universities, especially in Europe, HCI remains as a part of computer science.

- **Products, companies, industries:** One of the advantages that facilitated HCI research, is that the work is tied to an exponentially growing industry. The dramatic growth of the HCI discipline and the UXD profession was symbiotic with the exponential growth of chip speeds and decline of chip prices, which often led to breakthrough products that stimulated novel research directions. The synergy between HCI research and UXD innovations gave remarkable capabilities to huge numbers of users. The low-cost, convenient, and nearly instantaneous availability of music, photos, videos, e-commerce, email, and social media attracted huge audiences to laptop tools, web services, and mobile devices. Graphical user interfaces, web browsers, mobile devices, and social media were more than just interesting research topics: they were hot products from booming companies, engaged in intense competition. Corporate interest in HCI research results about menu design, touchscreens, or e-commerce engendered live seminars, video courses, satellite TV programs, and eventually tutorials. Leading companies and start-ups put these research results to work at scale to serve billions of users. Apple's design strength became a huge business story as it grew to be the most valued company in the world.

- **Best Paper Honors, Test-of-Time Awards, Academy Fellows:** As conferences expand to include dozens or hundreds of papers, conference committees recognize the benefits of choosing best papers or honorable mention awards to highlight exceptional work. Since prospective selections have not been shown to predict citation counts, a retrospective approach eventually gains support for the idea of awarding Test-of-Time Awards to the papers that 5 or 10 years after publication have been most influential. Other signs of disciplinary maturity are for professional societies to create an Academy or Fellows award, launch doctoral consortia, start video series, and sponsor design contests. Acceptance by other disciplines is signaled by election of leaders to National Academies of Science or Engineering or awards of honorary doctorates. HCI Pioneers in the U.S. National Academy of Engineering include Fred Brooks, Stuart Card, Susan Dumais, James Foley, Alan Kay, Sara Kiesler, Judy Olson, and me. HCI Pioneers who have received honorary doctorates include, at least, Tim Berners-Lee, Fred Brooks, Jack Carroll, Elizabeth Churchill, Gerhard Fischer, Alan Kay, Jaron Lanier, Allen Newell, Don Norman, Jimmy Wales, and me.

- **Book series, journals, magazines:** Sufficient interest in the new discipline encouraged publishers to support book series, edited by prominent leaders; soon enough, a respected leader and aspiring trailblazer gathered an editorial board for a professional peer-reviewed journal. Brian Gaines and colleagues made an important contribution in starting the *International Journal of Man-Machine Studies* in 1969, which eventually was renamed as the *International Journal of Human-Computer Studies*. Edited books and book series from academic and trade publishers gave authors opportunities to report on their work and readers a chance to learn about diverse perspectives. Edited books and book series from academic and trade publishers gave authors opportunities to report on their work and readers a chance to learn about diverse perspectives. Jack Carroll's contribution as a keen editor is notable for his helping to develop and refine paper collections in 14 books, serving as Editor-in-Chief of the *ACM Transactions Computer Human Interaction* (2003–2009), and editing the 40+ books in the series that offers this current book. Following contemporary practice, blogs, videos, and social media efforts followed. Sufficiently broad interest facilitated practitioner-oriented newsletters and magazines. A memorable occasion was when Brad Myers, Marilyn Mantei, Dave Kieras, and I, representing the SIGCHI-Executive Council, went to ACM Headquarters in 1993 to encourage the development of what would become the *ACM Interactions Magazine*.

There are certainly other components and strategies to paradigm births, but I hope this first attempt at listing the components needed to spawns new disciplines will receive a thorough historical or academic analysis. Future components for a mature field would be national and international recognition, maybe by having U.S. Department of User Experience Design and corporate Chief User Experience Officers. There is already an International Atomic Energy Agency, so why not an International User Experience Agency? Such agencies underline the potent effects of these technologies, ensure standards of practice, promote universal usability, and work to promote workforce readiness.

3.3   THREATS TO PARADIGM BIRTHS

Paradigm births and childhood can be perilous periods with threats to continued growth from external and internal forces. Pressures from related disciplines can suppress growth, capture emerging leaders, or make competitive attacks. All of these occurred in the case of HCI and UXD, such as termination of labs, curricula, or book series, but the community was strong enough to endure. Internal conflicts among competing journals, conferences, and universities also produced turbulence but no existential threats. The greatest threat has been from competing disciplines, where advocates were more effective in capturing media-driven public attention, such as computer graphics and AI.

As disciplines mature they accumulate a shared body of knowledge with an accepted set of research methods, but then there is a danger that fresh ideas will be rejected by established leaders. While a mature field benefits from cohesion, it also needs to support exploration at the frontiers and be open to new ideas, directions and research methods. The process of progressive differentiation spawned dozens of specialized conferences, including more than 30 that the ACM SIGCHI sponsors and more than 30 others that they cooperate with. Still the countervailing process of hierarchical integration means that the main annual CHI conference is a unifying event that consistently draws more than 3000 attendees. Related conferences such as HCI International, launched by Gavriel Salvendy in the mid-1980s, draw almost 2000 people annually with strong international participation. Salvendy ran these conferences in partnership with Michael J. Smith and later Constantine Stephanidis. While there were competitive overtones in having several large conferences, HCI and UXD continue to grow so there was room for multiple initiatives around conferences, journals, educational programs, etc.

3.4   CONCLUSION

The birth of the HCI paradigm produced fraternal twins: an academic discipline and UXD as a professional field. Tracking the trajectory of paradigm births and understanding the underlying components is a difficult job, but one that is worth doing to understand how different fields emerge or dissipate. New topics such as games with a purpose, citizen science, virtual/augmented reality, or sustainability bring in new problems, methods, and people. A network analysis that studies the growth of connections between disparate communities could reveal other insights. Improved quantitative data would help, especially to track movement of ideas, as would a clearer theory of what drives success or failure. A truly valuable theory, one that could guide promoters of future disciplines, would assess the role of individuals, universities, industry, and professional societies. A broader contextual analysis could evaluate how well new disciplines align with broader societal movements, economic conditions, and relevant cultural shifts.

Other analyses might indicate which combinations of components are necessary for successful paradigm births and which are merely optional. A final aspect of disciplinary success that is worthy of study is the role of the inspirational passion shown by leaders, intense energy invested by organizers, and astonishing creativity of devoted students.

CHAPTER 4

Future Possibilities

4.1   INTRODUCTION

The HCI Pioneers have much to be proud of. Their work has democratized access to technologies that enabled families and friends to be in closer touch, to offer assistance and empathy, and to form trusting compassionate relationships. The current and future generations of technology will give colleagues and neighbors tools to work together more effectively, while empowering citizens and markets to negotiate complex political, economic, and social realities. But maybe the greatest HCI contribution has been to support the powerful desire of individuals to be creative. Users of computers and mobile devices can more easily compose music, create art, produce videos, make inventions, initiate political movements, and start businesses. Like the biological Cambrian explosion, the current expansion of creative possibilities will have vast effects by enabling more people to be more creative, more of the time.

At the same time, these successes have brought new problems such as cybercrime, cyber-bullying, privacy violations, enabling of terrorism, easy proliferation of hate speech, fake news, and other pernicious uses. I worry about the cyber-obsessions of excessive game playing, reduced face-to-face human contact, and new digital divides. I'm also troubled by the infatuation of journalists who disseminate humanoid robot scenarios and AI fantasies that undermine our sense of what it means to be human. Other concerns are the loss of privacy and security, compounded by the bewildering complexity of e-commerce, business transactions, and government services. Could the next generation of technologies reduce the high levels of frustration that so many users, including me, experience on a daily basis? How could deeper discussions of ethics and responsibility educate developers to think more deeply about pro-social applications infused with the spirit of positive computing (Calvo and Peters, 2014)?

And yet, even with all these deep concerns, I believe in a hope-filled future in which improved applications support human connections, community building efforts, wellness/health, and sustainable ecosystems. In the conclusion of our 6th edition of *Designing the User Interface* (2016a) we offered 16 grand challenges for HCI researchers, which focused on specific research directions.

1. Develop a handbook of human needs.

2. Shift from user experience to community experience.

3. Refine theories of persuasion.

4. Encourage resource conservation.

5. Shape the learning health system.

6. Advance the design of medical devices.

7. Support successful aging strategies.

8. Promote lifelong learning.

9. Stimulate rapid interface learning.

10. Engineer new business models.

11. Design novel input and output devices.

12. Accelerate analytic clarity.

13. Amplify empathy, compassion, and caring.

14. Secure cyberspace.

15. Encourage reflection, calmness, and mindfulness.

16. Clarify responsibility and accountability.

There are undoubtedly other grand challenges that will address vital human needs. I think the most important topic to study is the continued growth in participation, cooperation, and collaboration through social media. These social media greatly lower the barriers to collaboration thereby promoting new forms of community, strategies for governance, and patterns of leadership. Effective design of social media applications has enabled many forms of citizen science, crowdsourced data gathering, and bottom-up fundraising for charitable (GoFundMe) and business purposes (Kick-Starter, Indiegogo). Social media have also opened up opportunities within the sharing economies (Uber, Lyft, and many more), chances to rent housing (Airbnb), and ways to start a small business (Etsy, TaskRabbit).

4.2   EMERGING TECHNOLOGIES FOR STILL GRANDER GOALS

I believe that new mobile device technologies for augmented reality will spread rapidly, while virtual reality will mature and find narrower audiences devoted to gaming and entertainment. A growing theme will be body sensors and actuators to support wellness/health, improved perceptual capabilities, and extended physical performance, especially for users with disabilities. Patient-collected medical, diet, and exercise data will eventually be integrated with physician-generated electronic health records to provide more complete analyses that promote wellness/health. Creativity support tools, such as the dramatically improved cellphone cameras, simplified video editing, and music composition suites enable more users to be more creative more of the time (I repeat this message because I think it is so important).

An admirable aspect of the HCI community has been its devotion to inclusive design or universal usability. By studying and respecting the needs of old and young, poor and rich, low and high literacy individuals, variously gendered users, speakers of diverse languages, and users with disabilities, researchers and developers have been able to produce products and services that are widely accessible. There is still room for progress, but the positive intentions of HCI community members has improved quality of life for most users, while enabling participation and increasing opportunities for many people (Fischer, 2018).

Another hope-filled direction is toward open systems that promote freely shared data, easily available research papers, open-source software, and freely accessible systems. While many organizations continue to have closed processes, the trend is toward openness.

HCI professionals also have demonstrated admirable aspirations such as raising awareness of the need for environmental preservation, changing lifestyles to promote energy sustainability, and using persuasive apps to support community safety. The United National Sustainable Development Goals (https://www.un.org/sustainabledevelopment/) are a good roadmap for HCI researchers and UX designers. These 17 grand goals are accompanied by 169 metrics meant to guide efforts toward the intended 2030 time horizon.

Grander goals include finding pathways to world peace, maybe by way of dispute mediation services, conflict management strategies, and deliberation tools. These strategies are based on the belief that all parties seek a peaceful resolution, but this is not always the case. Criminals, vandals, terrorists, and even legitimate governments may frustrate even the best-intentioned efforts. Similarly, conspiracy theorists, fake news promoters, hate groups, and bullies will adopt the latest technologies requiring ever-greater efforts to contain them.

4.3   SHIFTING TO FRONTIER THINKING

Still after all these concerns, I rely on the Enlightenment philosophy that reason, science, and humanism can lead to productive discussions that bring progress toward improved quality of life. I respect those who find the courage to design something bold, who crave to discover something new, and who unleash their passion to build something that helps people.

Humans are remarkable in their ability to invent something new by combining, altering, or extending existing technologies. Brian Arthur clearly described this process in *The Nature of Technology* (2009):

…new technologies were not "inventions" that came from nowhere. All the examples I was looking at were created—constructed, put together, assembled—from previously existing technologies. Technologies in other words consisted of other technologies, they arose as combinations of other technologies.

For example, computers were built on a long history of other innovations, but then computers were linked by Local Area Nets to support communication. Next, Vint Cerf and Bob Kahn wove these together into a network of networks using innovative packet-switching technology to create the internet. Then Tim Berners-Lee facilitated human use of the internet by inventing the World Wide Web. Technology entrepreneurs soon turned the Web into a foundation for their social media applications, which became advertising platforms that were employed by political operatives to influence elections and spread fake news.

I call this capacity *frontier thinking*, which suggests going beyond the known, familiar, and safe. It takes courage to move from the safety of familiar knowledge to take on the risks of the unknown, but the thrill of discovery and joy of invention drive the innovators forward (Isaacson, 2014). I claim that human activities often employ frontier thinking, which addresses highly varying situations where past experience is helpful, but innovative application of diverse skills is needed. Frontier situations are characterized by incomplete, inconsistent, or incorrect data, forcing risky choices, but inviting innovative solutions.

In the past, frontier thinking was seen as the province of a small number of celebrated thinkers, such as Leonardo, Einstein, Marie Curie, or Rachel Carson. Even recent brilliant innovators, such as Apple leader Steve Jobs, political organizer Jody Williams, film producer Stephen Spielberg, or women's rights activist Malala Yousafzai, were portrayed as unique.

However, I see that more people are taking on creative challenges using innovative apps, such as organizing political movements with EveryAction, launching start-up companies with Kickstarter, or leading charitable projects with GoFundMe. I think the democratization of creativity is this century's most powerful force. The unbounded human capacity for bringing people together to do something new can address the challenges we face in quelling social turmoil, nurturing wellness/health, and preserving ecosystems.

Those who fear that automation will produce widespread unemployment have clearly misunderstood human capacities for reinvention. The disruptions from change have always been difficult and remain a challenge for those whose skills are no longer needed, but the opportunities for individuals to retrain, learn about new jobs, and start a business of their own have never been greater. While government and business-funded projects are needed, widely used educational resources such as Coursera and entrepreneurial platforms such as Airbnb, Etsy, eBay, or TaskRabbit enable bottom-up innovation, part-time work, and small-business opportunities.

Beyond personal initiative, the current set of rich social media tools provide more opportunities for reporting on and giving recognition to inspirational teachers, compassionate nurses, barrier-breaking athletes, ardent musicians, and impassioned inventors. Social media postings raise awareness of what is possible and give innovators feedback to redirect their efforts.

Even small creative contributions help authors strengthen their skills, enable readers to improve their lives, and assist community organizers in generating constructive participation. These small steps include taking the initiative to write thoughtful reviews for books, movies, and restaurants, produce educational videos to help people carry out home-improvement projects, or create new lesson plans that feature active learning and team projects. Over time, proficiency in writing, making videos, or teaching students build confidence in frontier thinkers' skills, which eventually mature into more elaborate capabilities. The success of Wikipedia is a remarkable demonstration of the power of well-designed technology to provide strong social support for readers, contributors, collaborators, and leaders. Algorithms can make minor edits and reduce vandalism, but the process of building Wikipedia is a distinctly human experience, which can be seen in the intense enthusiasm and joyous encounters at the annual Wikimania conference.

HCI researchers could develop even more powerful tools, which support these and other forms of frontier thinking. Improved tools could provide potent search capabilities to find exceptional performances of pilots in difficult situations, patients who did better than predicted, and patterns of effective political organizing that lead to successful outcomes. Frontier thinking tools would give access to rich models that users could manipulate to explore how variables change in diverse contexts and how pushing past established limits would lead to new possibilities. For all the advances in technology, I see vital distinctions between what people can do and what machines can do. As time goes by, I believe observers will see ever more clearly that people are not computers and computers are not people. Human capabilities will be valued, human responsibility will be respected, and technology developers will shift toward tool-like designs with effective user interfaces that ensure human control.

I have been fortunate to live though a time of enormous changes and contribute to several technology-mediated societal transformations. I am proud of what I, and the community that includes the HCI Pioneers, have accomplished, but troubled by the problems we have created. The harsh reality of endless problems pushes me to work ever more diligently with like-minded and well-intentioned people who find meaning in trying to make a better world. There is lots of work to be done, so let's get on with it. It may be a romantic belief, but I remain an optimist, hopeful that, on average, tomorrow will be a better day.

CHAPTER 5

About the HCI Pioneers Project

I have had the pleasure of meeting and being inspired by many of the researchers and innovators who contributed to the emergence of HCI. They were memorable for their thoughtful research, innovative systems, energetic lectures, passionate discussions, and personal warmth. This Personal Photo Journal is intended as a tribute to these individuals and as a celebration of their contributions to HCI. The initial implementation was as a website (http://hcipioneers.wordpress.com), and now a selection of the photos and text appears in this book.

- **HCI Pride:** While the advances in technology brought about by Moore's Law continue to have a dramatic impact on computing, so have the remarkable contributions of HCI. The astonishing success of 7 billion users of mobile devices is due to the devoted work of user interface researchers and designers who enabled participation by novices and experts, children and older adults, as well as users with diverse language needs and a variety of abilities. Excellent design enables users to carry out life-critical tasks, to be effective in professional situations, and to enjoy games, media, and better communication capabilities. Well-designed user interfaces support users in delivering better healthcare, safer transportation, improved education, and more. At the same time, advanced user interfaces enable skilled professionals to collaborate more widely, explore deeper creative possibilities, and make increasingly vital discoveries.

- **Goal:** My goal in creating this journal is to celebrate the thriving research community that has propelled the HCI field and to make their work visible to a wider audience. I have written my personal appreciation for each of the luminaries, hoping to say something unique and descriptive of their impact. I think the social processes by which ideas are communicated are fascinating—some researchers proudly promoted their ideas to large audiences while others cautiously explain them and seek feedback from trusted colleagues. Big lectures, seminar-style gatherings, or personal dinner table discussions are all interesting to me, especially the participants' facial expressions, body language, and hand movements. Capturing the transmission of an idea is difficult; ideas, like neutrinos, are invisible except for the effect they have on others.

- **Choices and biases:** My choice of researchers and designers to include in this tribute was guided by my encounters at conferences, so there is a bias toward those who work on topics close to my own interests. There is likewise a bias toward those working in North America because that is where most of the conferences I attended were hosted.

I used the CHI Fellow Awards page as further guidance to select researchers who have gained recognition from our professional community. My selections were also biased toward those I have worked with at the University of Maryland's Human-Computer Interaction Lab. I also included some influential personalities, such as Douglas Engelbart, Tim Berners-Lee, J. C. R. Licklider, and Jimmy Wales, who were outside the CHI community. There are many other important contributors to the field who I have not photographed and many that I have not yet included—this is a work in progress and I hope to add more researchers to the website over time. I am solely responsible for the choice of who is included, and hope to include other contributors as time and resources permit.

- **Permissions:** I believe that these photos were taken at public, professional events, so I have not asked permission to publish them on this site, but in three years on the Web, no requests came to me about removing photos. I have been in contact with most of the those profiled, who are still alive, to give them an opportunity to comment and fix their profiles. These photos are freely available for personal use, although I appreciate a simple credit such as "Photo by Ben Shneiderman." I reserve the copyright on these photos, so those interested in using the photos on the web, in print, in video, or other media for educational or commercial purposes should contact me (ben@cs.umd.edu). We worked hard to document the location, date, and people in the photos, as well as background information, but please help us correct any errors.

- **Team:** The *Encounters with HCI Pioneers* website was built over the summer of 2015 by Catherine Bloom and Sarah Sexton. During the fall of 2015 and into 2016, Sarah Sexton and Gowtham Ashok continued the effort to add more pioneers. They worked hard to collect accurate historical information and write short strong summaries. Earlier work on organizing and annotating my photo archives was done by Veysel Cetiner, Amanda Pirner, Walden Davis, and Chelsea Clarke. I greatly appreciate all their work. Thanks especially to Jennifer Preece, Catherine Plaisant, and Ben Bederson for their comments and guidance about the website.

Catherine Bloom   Sarah Sexton   Gowtham Ashok

- **Press Coverage:** It's been great to get widespread attention for this project:

  - *New York Times*, Steve Lohr, September 7, 2015

  - **Eager Eyes**, Robert Kosara, September 1, 2015

  - **Transforming Grounds**, Erik Stolterman, September 2, 2015

  - **CMU HCI Institute** website. September 2, 2015

  - **Norman-Nielsen Group**, September 8, 2015

  - **Susan Dray** blog, September 9, 2015

  - **Joelle Coutaz** lab website, March 7, 2016

  - **CRA CCC Blog**, March 21, 2016

- **Related:** While this Personal Photo Journal focuses on HCI Pioneers, for those interested in computer scientists and researchers in related fields, please see my photos of 22 Computer Pioneers, at the Computer History Museum website—4 of those are included in this website. There are other worthwhile resources, such as Tamara Adlin's website on User Experience (UX) Pioneers and Brad Myers' "A Brief History of Human Computer Interaction Technology."

- **Technology:** Around 2000, I received funding from the ACM SIGCHI to scan my paper prints and color slides, which became the core of the 3,300 photos at the 2001 conference that produced the ACM SIGCHI Photo History (Shneiderman et al. 2002). The resolution of these early scans could be improved, but that remains a future project. The early prints, negatives, and slides were shipped in August 2018 to the Charles Babbage Institute (CBI) at the University of Minnesota in Minneapolis. As the leading archive for computing history, they will provide a long-term home for these materials, while making them accessible to students, researchers, journalists, and others. Archivist Amanda Wick and Director Jeffrey Yost were warmly supportive to CBI's taking on this collection.

  As I moved to digital cameras, the early images had low resolution, but over time the image quality improved. I used a digital single lens reflex for special events, but often I just used a good quality pocket camera that was easy to carry. By 2015, high quality smartphone cameras became good enough that even my pocket camera often stayed home. Of course, I like the higher quality images, but often the pocket camera and increasingly the smartphone camera was what I used to record fortuitous encounters.

  The March/April 2007 issue of *ACM Interactions* has an 8-page portfolio of 100+ photos from the 25-year history of ACM CHI conferences. The MyLifePix archive (2007) of 12,000 photos (scanned and born digital images) are partially indexed by name, date, and location. I have long worked on photo management tools, presentations strategies, and websites, including development of the Photofinder and PhotoMesa tools, and the BRQ photo presentation tool.

- **My uncle's inspiration:** My devotion to photography is inspired by my uncle David Seymour (1911–1956, known as "Chim"), a world-famous photojournalist, who was a founder of the legendary photography collective, Magnum Photos (https://www.magnumphotos.com/photographer/david-seymour/). The International Center of Photography hosts much of his work and presents occasional exhibits of his work (http://www.icp.org/chim), while current information on other exhibits around the world and publications is on another website (http://www.davidseymour.com).

- **Publication as a monograph:** Each HCI Pioneer profile was produced as a two-page spread in this book, forcing a further selection of photographs and text. Readers are encouraged to visit the website to see the full profile. Publication in print form, as well as distribution by PDF files, brings me additional satisfaction since these creative contributors to HCI research will become more widely known.

Table of Abbreviations and Acronyms

- Artificial Intelligence (AI)

- Association for Computing Machinery (ACM)

- Computer Human Interaction (CHI)

- Graphic User Interfaces (GUIs)

- Human–Computer Interaction (HCI)

- Human Sciences and Advanced Technology (HUSAT) Research Institute

- International Federation for Information Processing (IFIP)

- iSchools (Information Schools)

- Massively Open Online Courses (MOOCs)

- National Aeronautics and Space Administration (NASA)

- National Science Foundation (NSF)

- Query-by-Example (QBE)

- Structured Query Language (SEQUEL) (later SQL)

- Special Interest Group for Computer-Human Interaction (Association for Computing Machinery, ACM) SIGCHI.

- Stanford Research Institute (SRI)

- Usability Professionals Association (UPA), predecessor of the User Experience Professionals Association

- User interface/eXperience Design (UXD)

- "What You See Is What You Get" (WYSIWYG)

- Windows, icons, menus, and pointing devices (WIMPs)

- Xerox Palo Alto Research Center (PARC)

References

Arthur, Brian. (2009). *The Nature of Technology: What It Is and How It Evolves*, Free Press, New York. 47

Barkhuus, Louise and Rode, Jennifer. (2007). From Mice to Men – 24 Years of Evaluation. *Proceedings SIGCHI Conference on Human Factors in Computing Systems (CHI 2007)*, ACM Press, New York. DOI: 10.1145/1240624.2180963. 26, 35

Bartneck, Christoph and Hu, Jun. (2009). Scientometric analysis of the CHI proceedings. *Proceedings SIGCHI Conference on Human Factors in Computing Systems (CHI 2009)*, ACM Press, New York, 699–708. DOI: 10.1145/1518701.1518810. 26, 35

Bennett, John L. (1972). The user interface interactive systems. In C. Cuadra (Ed.), *Annual Review of Information Science and Technology 7*, American Society for Information Science, Washington, DC 159–196. 6

Bush, Vannevar. (1945). As we may think, *Atlantic Monthly* 176, 1, 105–108. 1

Calvo, Rafael A. and Peters, Dorian. (2014).*Positive Computing: Technology for Well-Being and Human Potential*, MIT Press: Cambridge MA, 45

Carbonell, Jaime, Elkind, J. I., and Nickerson, Ray. (1968). Importance of time in a time-sharing system, *Human Factors* 10, 2. DOI: 10.1177/001872086801000205. 4

Card, Stuart, Moran, Thomas, and Newell Allen. (1983). *The Psychology of Human-Computer Interaction*, Lawrence Erlbaum Associates, Hillsdale, NJ. 11, 38

Chapanis, Alphonse. (1975). Interactive human communication, *Scientific American* 232, 3, 36–42. DOI: 10.1038/scientificamerican0375-36. 6

Churchill, Elizabeth, Bowser, Anne, and Preece, Jennifer. (2013). Teaching and learning human-computer interaction: past, present, and future, *ACM Interactions* 20, 2, 44–53, http://dl.acm.org/citation.cfm?id=2427086. DOI: 10.1145/2427076.2427086. 38

Eason, Ken. (1976). Understanding the naive computer user, *The Computer Journal* 19, 1, 3–7, DOI: 10.1093/comjnl/19.1.3. 8

Edmonds, Ernest A. and Lee, J. (1974). An appraisal of some problems of achieving fluid man-machine interaction, *Proceedings EUROCOMP'74*, Online Computing Systems, 635–645. 37

Engel, Stephen E. and Granda, Richard E. (1975). Guidelines for Man/Display Interfaces, Technical Report TR 00.2720, IBM, Poughkeepsie, NY. 6

Engelbart, Douglas C. and English, William K. (1968). A research center for augmenting human intellect, AFIPS *Proceedings Fall Joint Computer Conference* 33, 395–410. DOI: 10.1145/1476589.1476645. 3

Fischer, Gerhard. (2018). Design trade-offs for Quality of Life, *ACM Interactions* XXV.1, 26–33. 47

Foley, James and Wallace, Victor L. (1974). The art of graphic man-machine conversation, *Proceedings of the IEEE*, 62, 4. DOI: 10.1109/PROC.1974.9450. 6

Gaines, Brian R. and Facey, Peter V. (1975). Some experience in interactive system development and applications, *Proceedings of the IEEE*, 63, 6, 894–911. DOI: 10.1109/PROC.1975.9854. 8

Gold, Michael M. (1969). Time-sharing vs. batch processing: An experimental comparison of their values in a problem solving situation, *Communications of the ACM*, 12, 5, 249–259. DOI: 10.1145/362946.362958. 4

Grant, E. E., and Sackman, Harold. (1967). An exploratory investigation of programmer performance under on-line and off-line conditions. *IEEE Transactions on Human Factors in Electronics*, (1), 33-48. 4

Grodal, Stine, Gotsopoulos, Aleksios, and Suarez, Fernando F. (2015). The coevolution of technologies and categories during industry emergence, *Academy of Management Review* 40, 3, 423–445. DOI: 10.5465/amr.2013.0359. 35

Grudin, Jonathan. (2009). AI and HCI: Two Fields Divided by a Common Focus, *AI Magazine*, 48–57. DOI: 10.1609/aimag.v30i4.2271.

Grudin, Jonathan. (2016). *From Tool to Partner: The Evolution of Human-Computer Interaction*, Synthesis Lectures on Human-Centered Informatics, Morgan & Claypool Publishers, San Rafael, CA. DOI: 10.2200/S00745ED1V01Y201612HCI035. 26, 35

Guha, Shion, Steinhardt, Stephanie, Ahmed, Syed I., and Lagoze, Carl. (2013). Following bibliometric footprints: the ACM digital library and the evolution of computer science, *Proceedings 13th ACM/IEEE-CS Joint Conference on Digital Libraries*, 139–142. DOI: 10.1145/2467696.2467732. 35

Hansen, Wilfred J. (1971). User engineering principles for interactive systems, *Proceedings Fall Joint Computer Conference 39*, AFIPS Press, Montvale, NJ, 523–532. DOI: 10.1145/1479064.1479159. 6

Henry, Nathalie, Goodell, Howard, Elmqvist, Niklas and Fekete, Jean-Daniel (2007). 20 years of four HCI conferences: A visual exploration, *International Journal of Human-Computer Interaction*, 23:3, 239–285, DOI: 10.1080/10447310701702402. 26, 35

Hewett, Thomas, Baecker, Ronald, Card, Stuart, Carey, Tom, Gasen, Jean, Mantei, Marilyn, Perlman, Gary, Strong, Gary, and Verplank, William. (1992). *ACM SIGCHI Curricula for Human-Computer Interaction*, ACM Press, NY. DOI: 10.1145/2594128. 38

Hiltz, Starr Roxanne and Turoff, Murray. (1978). *The Network Nation: Human Communication via Computer*, Addison-Wesley Publishing Co., Reading, MA. 6

Hutchins, Edwin L., Hollan, James D. and Norman, Donald A. (1986). Direct manipulation interfaces. In D. A. Norman and S. W. Draper (Eds.), *User Centered System Design*, Lawrence Erlbaum:Mahwah, NJ, 87–124. 11

Institution of Electrical Engineers. (1982). *Man-Machine Systems: Proceedings of the International Conference*, Manchester, UK, IEE Publication Ser., No. 212. 39

Isaacson, Walter. (2014). *The Innovators: How a Group of Hackers, Geniuses, and Geeks Created the Digital Revolution*, Simon & Schuster, NY. 48

Kay, Alan and Goldberg, Adele. (1977). Personal dynamic media, *IEEE Computer* 10, 3, 31–41. DOI: 10.1109/C-M.1977.217672. 10

Koved, Larry and Shneiderman, Ben. (1986). Embedded menus: Selecting items in context, *Communications of the ACM* 29, 4. DOI: 10.1145/5684.5687. 14

Kuhn, Thomas. (1962). *The Structure of Scientific Revolutions*, University of Chicago Press, Chicago, IL (3rd edition 1996). 35

Licklider, Joseph C. R., (1960). Man-computer symbiosis, *IEEE Transactions on Human Factors in Electronics HFE-1*, 4–11. DOI: 10.1109/THFE2.1960.4503259. 2, 37

Martin, James. (1973). *Design of Man-Computer Dialogues*, Prentice-Hall, Inc., Englewood Cliffs, NJ, 4

Meadow, Charles T. (1970). *Man-Machine Communication*, Wiley-Interscience, New York.

Miller, Robert. (1968). Response time in man-computer conversational transactions, *Proceedings Spring Joint Computer Conference* 33, 267–277. DOI: 10.1145/1476589.1476628. 4

Myers, Brad A. (1998). A brief history of human computer interaction technology, *ACM Interactions* 5, 2, 44–54. http://www.cs.cmu.edu/~amulet/papers/uihistoryinteractions.pdf. DOI: 10.1145/274430.274436. 26, 29, 35

National Research Council's (NRC's) Computer Science and Telecommunications Board (CSTB) (1995). *Evolving the High Performance Computing and Communications Initiative to Sup-*

port the Nation's Information Infrastructure. The National Academies Press, Washington, DC. https://tinyurl.com/ycf47b3d. 29

National Research Council (2003). Computer Science and Telecommunications Board; Division on Engineering and Physical Sciences. *Innovation in Information Technology*. The National Academies Press, Washington, DC. https://www.nap.edu/catalog/10795/innovation-in-information-technology. 29, 35

National Research Council (2012). Committee on Depicting Innovation in Information Technology; Computer Science and Telecommunications Board; Division on Engineering and Physical Sciences. *Continuing Innovation in Information Technology*, The National Academies Press, Washington, DC. https://www.nap.edu/catalog/13427/continuing-innovation-in-information-technology. 29, 35

Nelson, Theodor. (1973). A conceptual framework for man-machine everything, *Proceedings of the National Computer Conference* 42, AFIPS Press, Montvale, NJ. DOI: 10.1145/1499586.1499776. DOI: 10.1145/1499586.1499776. 6

Nichols, Jean and Schneider, Michael. (1982). *Proceeding of the Conference on Human Factors in Computing Systems*, ACM, New York. http://dl.acm.org/citation.cfm?id=800049. 39

Norman, Donald A. and Draper, Stephen W. (1986). *User Centered Systems Design: New Perspective on Human-Computer Interaction*, Lawrence Erlbaum Associates, Hillsdale, NJ. DOI: 10.1201/b15703. 38

Norman, Donald A. (2013). *The Design of Everyday Things: Revised and Expanded Edition*, Basic Books, New York. 38

Pew, Richard. (2007). An Unlikely HCI Frontier— The Social Security Administration in 1978, *ACM Interactions*, 18-21. DOI: 10.1145/1242421.1242437. 8

Preece, Jennifer, Rogers, Yvonne, and Sharp, Helen. (2019). *Interaction Design: Beyond Human-Computer Interaction*, Wiley. 38

Raben, Joseph, Borman, Lorraine, Fenchel, Robert S., Ohlgren, Thomas H., Sondheimer, Norman K., Beveridge, Andrew A., and Roddy, Kevin. (1981). *Proceedings of the Joint Conference on Easier and More Productive Use of Computer Systems*, ACM Press, New York. 39

Reisner, Phyllis, Boyce, Raymond, and Chamberlin, Don. (1975). Human factors evaluation of two data base query languages, *Proceedings of the National Computer Conference* 44, AFIPS Press, Montvale, NJ. DOI: 10.1145/1499949.1500036. 8

Rogers, Yvonne. (2012). *HCI Theory: Classical, Modern, and Contemporary*, Synthesis Lectures on Human-Centered Informatics, Morgan & Claypool Publishers, San Rafael, CA.

Sackman, Harold. (1970). *Man-Computer Problem Solving: Experimental Evaluation of Time-Sharing and Batch Processing*. Auerbach Publ., Princeton, NJ. 4

Shackel, Brian. (1962). Ergonomics in the design of a large digital computer console. *Ergonomics*, 5, 229–241. DOI: 10.1080/00140136208930578. 37

Shackel, Brian. (1991). Usability—Context, framework, definition, design and evaluation. In B. Shackel and S. J. Richardson, (eds) *Human Factors for Informatics Usability*, Cambridge University Press. 8

Sharp, Helen, Rogers, Yvonne, and Preece, Jennifer. (2019). *Interaction Design: Beyond Human-Computer Interaction: Fifth Edition*, Wiley. 38

Sheridan, Thomas Ben, and Ferrel, William R. (1974). *Man-Machine Systems: Information, Control, and Decision Models of Human Performance*, MIT Press, Cambridge, MA. 6

Shneiderman, Ben. (1974). A computer graphics system for polynomials, *The Mathematics Teacher* 67,2, 111–113. 10

Shneiderman, Ben. (1975). Experimental testing in programming languages: Stylistic considerations and design techniques, *Proceedings National Computer Conference*, AFIPS Press, Montvale, NJ 653–656. DOI:10.1145/1499949.1500087. 4

Shneiderman, B. (1976). Applying the results of human factors experiments: Programming languages and data base query languages, *Proceedings Symposium on the Role of Human Factors in Computers*, R.E. Granda and J.M. Finkelman, Editors, The Human Factors Society, 51–58. 8

Shneiderman, Ben. (1982). Human factors experiments in designing interactive systems, *IEEE Computer* 12, 12 (December 1979), 9–19. Reprinted in Larson, J. A. (Editor), *Tutorial: End User Facilities in the 1980s*, IEEE Computer Society Press 16–26. 25

Shneiderman, Ben. (1980). *Software Psychology: Human Factors in Computer and Information Systems*, Little, Brown and Co. (formerly Winthrop Publ.), Boston, MA. 35, 38

Shneiderman, Ben. (1984). Book Review: The Psychology of Human-Computer Interaction. *Datamation* 30, 236–237. 11

Shneiderman, Ben. (1986). No members, no officers, no dues: A ten-year history of the Software Psychology Society, *ACM SIGCHI Bulletin* 18, 2 (October). http://dl.acm.org/citation.cfm?doid=15683.15685. 9, 26, 39

Shneiderman, Ben. (1987). *Designing the User Interface: Strategies for Effective Human-Computer Interaction*, Addison-Wesley Publ. Co., Reading, MA. 38

Shneiderman, Ben. (1993a). Supporting the process of innovation: The Maryland Way, In *Sparks of Innovation in Human-Computer Interaction* (B. Shneiderman, Editor), Ablex Pub., Norwood, NJ, 1-10. http://www.cs.umd.edu/hcil/pubs/books/maryland-way.shtml. 9

Shneiderman, Ben. (1993b). Declaration in Apple vs. Microsoft/Hewlett-Packard, In *Sparks of Innovation in Human-Computer Interaction* (B. Shneiderman, Editor), Ablex Publishers, Norwood, NJ, 355–361. 14

Shneiderman, Ben. (2007). 25 years of CHI conferences: Capturing the exchange of ideas, *ACM Interactions* XIV, 2, 24–31. Photo history with 100+ images. DOI: 10.1145/1229863.1229865. 54

Shneiderman, Ben. (2016). *The New ABCs of Research: Achieving Breakthrough Collaborations*, Oxford University Press.

Shneiderman, Ben (2017). Revisiting the astonishing growth of human–computer interaction research, *IEEE Computer* 50, 10 (October 2017), 8–11. http://ieeexplore.ieee.org/document/8057312/. 25, 36

Shneiderman, Ben, Dunne, Cody, Sharma, Puneet, and Wang, Ping. (2011). Innovation trajectories for information visualization: A comparison of treemaps, cone trees, and hyperbolic trees, *Information Visualization Journal* 11, 2, 87–105. DOI: 10.1177/1473871611424815. 22

Shneiderman, Ben, Kang, H., Kules, Ben, Plaisant, Catherine, Rose, A., and Rucheir, R. (2002). A photo history of SIGCHI: evolution of design from personal to public, *ACM Interactions* 9, 3, 17–23. DOI: 10.1145/506671.506682. 54

Shneiderman, Ben. and Maes, Pattie. (1997). Direct manipulation vs. software agents: A debate, *ACM Interactions* 4, 6, 42–61. 12

Shneiderman, Ben, Norman, Kent, Plaisant, Catherine, Bederson, Ben, Druin, Allison, and Golbeck, Jennifer. (2013). 30 Years at the University of Maryland's Human-Computer Interaction Lab (HCIL), *ACM Interactions* 20, 5, 50–57. http://dl.acm.org/citation.cfm?id=2508061. 10, 39

Shneiderman, Ben, Plaisant, Catherine, Cohen, Maxine, Jacobs, Steven, and Elmqvist, Niklas. (2016a). *Designing the User Interface: Strategies for Effective Human-Computer Interaction: Sixth Edition*, Pearson. 45

Shneiderman, Ben, Plaisant, Catherine, Cohen, Maxine, Jacobs, Steven, Elmqvist, Niklas, and Diakopoulos, Nicholas. (2016b). Grand Challenges in HCI, *ACM Interactions* 23, 5, 24–25. DOI: 10.1145/2977645. 26

Sime, M. E., Green, T. R. G., and Guest, D. J. (1973). Psychological evaluation of two conditional constructions used in computer languages, *International Journal of Man–Machine Studies* 5, 1 123–143. DOI: 10.1016/S0020-7373(73)80011-2. 8

Smith, Sidney L. and Mosier, Jane N. (1986). Guidelines for Designing User Interface Software, ESD-TR-86-278. http://www.hcibib.org/sam. DOI: 10.21236/ADA177198. 38

Sterling, Ted. (1974). Guidelines for humanizing computerized information systems, *Communications of the ACM* 17, 11, 609–613. DOI: 10.1145/361179.361180. 8

Sutherland, Ivan. (1963). Sketchpad, a man-machine graphical communications system, *Proceedings Spring Joint Computer Conference 1963*, Spartan Books, New York, 329–346. DOI: 10.1177/003754976400200514. 4

Thomas, John C. and Gould, John D. (1975). A psychological study of query by example, *Proceedings of the National Computer Conference* 44, AFIPS Press, Montvale, NJ. DOI: 10.1145/1499949.1500035. 8

University of Michigan School of Information: https://www.si.umich.edu/aboutsi/history-and-mission. 39

Van Dam, Andries. (1966). Computer driven displays and their use in man/machine interaction, *Advances in Computers* 7, Alt, F. L. and Rubinoff, M. (Editors), Academic Press, New York, 239-290. DOI: 10.1016/S0065-2458(08)60107-2. 4

Wasserman, Tony. (1973). The design of idiot-proof interactive systems, *Proceedings of the National Computer Conference* 42, AFIPS Press, Montvale, NJ. DOI: 10.1145/1499586.1499779. 6

Weinberg, Gerald M. (1971). *The Psychology of Computer Programming*, Van Nostrand Reinhold, New York. 4

Weizenbaum, Joseph. (1966). ELIZA - A computer program for the study of natural language communication between man and machine, *Communications of the ACM* 9, 1. 36-45. DOI: 10.1145/365153.365168. 6

Wiener, Norbert. (1954). *The Human Use of Human Beings: Cybernetics and Society*, Doubleday, New York, (1950), with revised edition in 1968. 8

Zloof, Moshe M. (1975). Query by example. In Proceedings of the May 19-22, 1975, National Computer Conference and Exposition, ACM. (pp. 431–438). 8

Part 2: HCI Pioneers Photo Journal

RON BAECKER
ICON INNOVATOR

Ron productively bridged the graphics and HCI communities, promoting animation and other strategies to convey insights, such as in his famed video comparing sorting algorithms. Later in his career, Ron admirably studied older adults and users with disabilities. Ron worked hard and has a long history of inspiring University of Toronto students and many of the rest of us.

– Ben Shneiderman

Ron Baecker is a prolific researcher and educator whose long career has produced innovations in a wide spectrum of fields, from computer graphics to responsibility and ethics in HCI to the development of using an icon for a cursor. He holds two patents in the display of computer-generated objects and has produced more than 100 books, articles, and instructional videos in addition to educating dozens of innovators in the field of HCI. His new book is *Computers and Society: Modern Perspectives* (OUP, 2019).

Baecker and Joanna McGrenere at the ACM Conference on Universal Usability in Arlington, VA, November 15–17, 2000.

His recent work includes founding the Technologies for Ageing Gracefully Lab, which seeks to develop "mental prostheses" to assist older adults and support autonomy through carefully designed interfaces and software structures. Baecker was elected to the SIGCHI Academy in 2005, made a Fellow of the ACM in 2011, and given the Lifetime Achievement Award from the Canadian Association of Computer Science in 2015.

Ron Baecker and Ron Baecker at the ACM CHI Conference on Human Factors in Computing Systems in Toronto, Canada on April 26, 2014.

Affiliations:

➤ Founder and Director, Technologies for Aging Gracefully Lab (2008–Present), Principal Researcher, Technology Research Center (1990–Present), Professor of Computer Science (1972–Present), University of Toronto

➤ Affiliate Scientist, Kunin-Lunenfeld Applied Research Unit. Baycrest Centre for Geriatric Care, Toronto (2004–Present)

➤ Bell University Laboratories Chair in Human-Computer Interaction (2002–2011)

➤ Founder and Chief Scientist, Knowledge Media Design Institute (1999–Present)

➤ Founder and CEO, Expresto Software Corp. (May 1998–October 2002)

Links:

➤ TAGlab

➤ University of Toronto

➤ Wikipedia

MICHEL BEAUDOUIN-LAFON
HCI TRAILBLAZER IN FRANCE

Michel Beaudouin-Lafon has admirably promoted HCI research in France, especially by founding the French Association Francophone d'Interaction Homme-Machine (AFIHM) and serving as its first president. His leadership in research propelled the Laboratoire de Recherche en Informatique (LRI) at the Universite Paris-Sud to international recognition. Michel worked hard to raise interest in HCI and often took French as well as international leadership positions. His style is quiet, but effective, making him a major contributor. Michel and his wife, Wendy Mackay, make a powerful team.

– Ben Shneiderman

Michel Beaudouin-Lafon is a Professor of Computer Science at Université Paris-Sud and a senior member of the Institut Universitaire de France. He has worked in HCIn for more than 30 years and played a fundamental role in establishing and promoting the discipline in France.

Beaudouin-Lafon's research interests span novel interaction techniques, computer-supported cooperative work, and design and research methods in the field of HCI. Beaudouin-Lafon collaborated with Wendy Mackay to develop Touchstone, a platform for designing, implementing, and analyzing controlled experiments. He also contributed to the InterLiving project, which brought together an interdisciplinary team of researchers to consult with six families and create new technologies supporting co-located and long-distance communication among family members. During a two-year visit at the University of Aarhus in Denmark, Beaudouin-Lafon developed his personal project on instrumental interaction while contributing to the CPN2000 project. Instrumental interaction is a model that extends the principles of direct manipulation and describes graphical user interfaces in terms of "domain objects" and "interaction instruments," which mediate interactions between users and manipulated objects. The project continues to fuel much of Beaudouin-Lafon's current work.

Michel Beaudouin-Lafon with his wife, Wendy Mackay, and Atau Tanaka at the ACM CHI Conference on Human Factors in Computing Systems in Vancouver, BC Canada in May 2011.

He served as director of LRI, the joint computer science laboratory of The French National Centre for Scientific Research (CNRS) and Université Paris-Sud. Today, LRI is one of the leading French labs dedicated to computer science and is internationally recognized in the area of HCI.

Affiliations:

- Full Professor, Université Paris-Sud (1997–Present)
- Senior Member, Institut Universitaire de France (2011–2016)
- Sabbatical Visitor, Stanford University (2010–2012)

Links:

- Homepage
- Wikipedia

BEN BEDERSON
ZOOMING PIONEER

Ben B's remarkable software engineering skills were productively applied to developing powerful toolkits such as Piccolo, implementing the International Children's Digital Library, and developing zooming strategies. We often differed on professional issues, but I always learned from Ben and respected his positions. Ben is a terrific colleague, so I was pleased to turn over the HCIL Directorship to him in 2000. One of my most satisfying professional accomplishments was attracting Allison Druin and Ben Bederson to our campus."

– Ben Shneiderman

Benjamin Bederson is a prolific researcher with diverse projects. His early work on zoomable user interfaces allowed for the development of Pad++ and Piccolo, which in turn led to the development of software like SpaceTree, DateLens, and PhotoMesa. Today, this work forms the core of such everyday tools as zoomable maps. He is also a co-founder of Zumobi, a mobile app company that partners with international premium brands to produce engaging content for diverse mobile devices.

Bederson and a young computer enthusiast at the ACM CHI Conference on Human Factors in Computing Systems in Vancouver, British Columbia, Canada in April 1996.

In 2010, Bederson and University of Maryland colleague Allison Druin created the International Children's Digital Library

(ICDL) for which they were awarded the 2010 ACM SIGCHI Social Impact Award. The ICDL is a unique resource that brings complex search functions to a juvenile audience and offers multiple search options, ranging from the common—age group and genre—to the uncommon—color of the book's cover.

His recent work has focused on human computation: "an approach to combine human with computational effort to solve problems at a scale and quality that neither could accomplish alone." One of these projects is MonoTrans, a collaborative translation project co-sponsored by the National Science Foundation and Google.

Myers (right) presenting Ben Bederson with the plaque commemorating his election to the CHI Academy during the ACM CHI Conference on Human Factors in Computing Systems in Austin, TX in May 2012.

Affiliations:

➤ Associate Provost of Learning Initiatives and Executive Director of the Teaching and Learning Transformation Center (2014–2018), Professor in the Department of Computer Science (1998–Present), University of Maryland, College Park

➤ Co-Founder, Hazel Analytics (2014–present)

➤ Co-Founder, Zumobi (2006–2014)

Links:

➤ UMD Website

➤ Wikipedia

TIM BERNERS-LEE
INVENTOR OF THE WORLD WIDE WEB

My occasional encounters with Tim led me to appreciate his devotion to creating a vibrant community (World Wide Web Consortium) that sets coding standards through rich deliberative processes. His 1989 manifesto for the Web thoughtfully laid out a bold vision that took the hypertext idea to a new level by allowing links to bring pages across the network from other computers. While I always appreciated his adopting and citing our HyperTies work on the selectable highlighted link, the Web's lack of two-way links seemed dangerous; but Tim demonstrated that the benefits of open linking were greater than the annoyance of an occasional 404 message about a missing page. I always admired his energy, technical savvy, and continuing commitment to making the Web work.

– Ben Shneiderman

Timothy "Tim" Berners-Lee is best known for building the World Wide Web. He began his work as the practical extrapolation of the theoretical works of Vannevar Bush and others. As he describes it, all the pieces were already in existence, "I just had to put them together."

Tim Berners-Lee makes his pitch at the First European Conference on Hypertext in Paris, France in November 1990.

The pieces of the Web that Berners-Lee assembled were the CERN Internet and Hypertext Markup Language (HTML) that allowed pages to be layered, connected, and readable by any computer that could connect via an internet browser.

Unlike some of his peers, Berners-Lee published his web tools without copyright or royalties to allow anyone with the skills and equipment to build web pages and expand the Web. In recent years, he has served as a vocal advocate for the Net Neutrality movement.

Tim Berners-Lee taking a photo while Wendy Hall smiles from the side at the Web Science workshop at MIT in November 2008 in Cambridge, MA.

Berners-Lee was knighted by Queen Elizabeth in 2004, listed by TIME Magazine among the 100 most influential people of the 20th century, and has received many awards for his work, including the ACM Turing Award in 2016.

Affiliations:

➤ Alliance for Affordable Internet (2013–Present)

➤ President, Open Data Institute (2012–Present)

➤ Adviser, Ford Foundation (2011–Present)

➤ Member, Power of Information Taskforce (2008–Present)

➤ Chair, Department of Computer Sciences, University of Southampton (2004–Present)

➤ Founder, World Wide Web Consortium and Foundation (1994–Present)

Links:

➤ Homepage at W3C

➤ Wikipedia

SARA BLY
USER STUDIES EXPERT AND CONSULTANT

Sara's early support for SIGCHI and her promotion of ethnographic approaches with qualitative data collection, especially in industry settings, helped advance our discipline. She managed the Collaborative Systems Group at PARC, where she initiated many projects that led to widely used collaboration tools. Sara's playful side was often on display at SIGCHI conferences. The SIGCHI Awards page sweetly and appropriately lists her as a "founding mother."

– Ben Shneiderman

Sara Bly's primary contribution to HCI has been in expanding the notion of user studies to include the context of an activity as well as the task itself. In the early 1980s, interaction studies were typically focused on usability studies. Working with others at Xerox PARC, Bly and her colleagues were one of the first groups of HCI designers and developers to combine their skills and perspectives with those of anthropologists and social scientists, such as Lucy Suchman, to conduct ethnographically informed fieldwork. This multi-modal approach has now become an accepted part of user experience studies to inform computer technology design and development.

Susan Dray (left) with Sara Bly at the ACM CHI Conference on Human Factors in Computing Systems in San Francisco, CA in April 1985.

At Xerox PARC, Bly was part of a team investigating the use of technology to enable people to connect in new ways, predating today's social media tools. The team based their work practice on the premise that technologies to support work activity are inexorably intertwined with the social setting and the nature of the work, as well as with the formal features of the technology itself.

The team's Media Space diverged from the video-conferencing of the 1980s to provide an "always-on" environment. From an HCI point of view, the significance was not in merely removing the requirement of premeditated action to "turn on" and "turn off" interactions. Rather, it provided a space that could support and facilitate observations and conversations as well as ad hoc collaborations in a more natural manner.

Sara Bly (center) with Andrew Fiore, Jennifer Preece, Ben Shneiderman, and Catherine Plaisant (left to right) at the ACM CHI Conference on Human Factors in Computing Systems in Minneapolis, MN in April 2002.

Affiliations:

➤ Sara Bly Consulting, User studies for Microsoft, Intel, FXPAL, etc. (1994–Present)

➤ Instructor, User-Centered Design, University of Toronto (2005)

Links:

➤ Homepage

➤ Interview Transcript

FRED BROOKS
OPERATING SYSTEMS AND SOFTWARE ENGINEERING DESIGN GURU

Fred Brooks remains a leader in software engineering and computer graphics. His 1975 book The Mythical Man Month *remains a best seller because of its insight-filled comments about the social processes involved in software development. He received the National Medal of Technology in 1985 and the ACM Turing Award in 1999. His smiling disposition and vigorous lecturing style were an attraction for me.*

– Ben Shneiderman

Frederick "Fred" Brooks is perhaps best known for his work managing the development of today's mainframe systems. He managed the hardware development of the IBM System/360 family of computers and then managed the development its OS/360 software in the early 1960s. System/360 is generally regarded as the first family of computers, in that a single architecture was migrated across the spectrum of use from personal to corporate, high to low-end, science to business.

Working under the direction of Bob O. Evans, Brooks and his colleagues developed the System/360, the first computer product line based on the 8-bit byte. The OS/360 was also an early adopter of Direct Access Storage Devices, such as hard disks, floppy discs or CDs, to expand the versatility of machines for diverse uses.

Fred Brooks (c) and colleagues at the CHI Conference on Human Factors in Computing in Boston, MA on April 13, 1986.

In 1975, Brooks published *The Mythical Man-Month* about the realities of designing software. In this book, he outlined what has become known as Brooks's Law, generally defined as "adding manpower to a late software project makes it later."

Fred Brooks and Doug Engelbart in dinner discussion at the Hypertext 1987 Conference in Chapel Hill, NC.

Affiliations:

- ➤ Founding Chair (1964–1984), Professor (1964–2015), University of North Carolina
- ➤ IBM (1956–1965)

Links:

- ➤ Wikipedia
- ➤ Homepage

BILL BUXTON
TOUCHSCREEN INNOVATOR

We need more Bill Buxton's in HCI. He started as a genuine rockstar—a real performing musician—and still gives the best performances of anyone in our field. He offers his incredibly detailed knowledge of input devices and strategies to whoever asks a good question. His eyes sparkle, his body moves, and Willy smiles with delight. He believes in the power of design and has taught me and others to respect and value it. I wish our life paths had given us more time to be together—he's so different from others I work with and such fun!

– Ben Shneiderman

William Arthur Stewart "Bill" Buxton's most prominent contribution to the field of HCI was the development of the multi-touch interface, such as the trackpad on a laptop and the fully interactive screen on iPads and other tablet computers. Buxton also contributed much of the background work to this innovation, including applying Fitts's Law, which explains how humans judge distances to targets. For example, when a computer user moves a mouse to navigate on a screen, the distance the user moves the mouse is not a true 1:1 ratio compared to how far the pointer moves on the screen. Buxton's work enabled optimal interface manipulation by perfecting the coordination between the physical input device, the mouse or the human hand in touch-screen devices, and the pointer within the machine.

Brad Myers, Bill Buxton, Terry Winograd, and Ron Baeker (left to right) at the ACM CHI Conference on Human Factors in Computing Systems in Portland, Oregon in April 2005.

In addition to this work, Buxton has also been a leading researcher for Microsoft, a regular contributor to Business Week, and the author of *Sketching User Experiences*. A dedicated supporter and contributor to the fine and performing arts, Buxton has developed several musical instruments. He is also a published author on the history of Canada.

Bill Buxton explains his exhibit of interaction devices at the ACM CHI Conference on Human Factors in Computing Systems in Vancouver, Canada in May 2011.

Affiliations:

> Principal Researcher, Microsoft (2004–Present)

> Owner, Gallery 888 (2000–2010)

> Board Member, Canadian Film Centre (1998–2004)

> Chief Scientist, SGI Inc. (1995–2002)

> Chief Scientist, Alias|Wavefront (now Autodesk, a SGI subsidiary) (1994–2002)

> Consulting Researcher, XeroxPARC (1989–1994)

Links:

> Homepage

> Wikipedia

STUART CARD
SEARCHING MODELER

Stu Card's capacity to fuse big ideas in psychology and computing have produced a steady flow of important books and papers. I had the pleasure to work with Stu and Jock Mackinlay on our 1999 book Readings in Information Visualization, *for which Stu supplied to potent subtitle* Using Vision to Think. *Working together was great fun as we blended our ideas to achieve "taxonomy harmony" and a balanced set of references to PARC's and HCIL's work. Stu could also be generous, as when he saw me after reading my 1982 direct manipulation paper—he pointed at me and said, "You got it!" His confirmation was worth a lot to me. I hope I've been as generous to him, because his work so often gets it right.*

– Ben Shneiderman

Stuart Card has made a wide range of contributions to the field of HCI, but his breakthroughs have stemmed from the conjunction of his background in psychology and his career in computing technologies.

Stuart Card (center), Jock Mackinlay, and Ben Shneiderman pose with their book at the ACM CHI Conference on Human Factors in Computing Systems in Fort Lauderdale, FL, April 5–10, 2003.

Card and Peter Pirolli's collaborative work on information foraging is seminal in the field of HCI, because it is describes how humans search for, take in, and subsequently adapt or abandon strategies for seeking information based on their successes or failures. This work not only informs the spectrum of hardware and software development, but is also widely discussed in the Information Sciences.

Stuart Card (left), Peter Pirolli, and Jennifer Preece at an ACM CHI Conference on Human Factors in Computing Systems in Vancouver in 2011..

Like Bill Buxton, Card also worked on the application of Fitts' Law to computer input devices, focusing on the mouse. In addition, he co-authored *The Psychology of Human-Computer Interaction* with Allen Newell and Thomas P. Moran. The book lays out the GOMS model, an elementary model upon which dozens of industry-specific models have been based. His second book, *Readings in Information Visualization: Using Vision to Think,* co-authored with Jock D. Mackinlay and Ben Shneiderman, collects and explains the original research in the field of information visualization and its universal applicability.

Affiliations:

➤ Consulting Professor (previously adjunct faculty), Stanford University

➤ Senior Research Fellow, User Interface Research Group, XeroxPARC (1974–2010)

Links:

➤ Wikipedia

➤ National Academy of Engineering Profile

➤ The Franklin Institute Profile

JACK CARROLL
A FOUNDING FATHER OF HCI

The ways in which Jack Carroll applied his psychology background to creatively describe user behavior helped make HCI a respected discipline. Jack's early paper on the Task–Artefact Cycle was a clever and surprising insight into how users worked on tasks, which led to ever more effective user interfaces. Jack can crack a smile, but he's often very work-focused. His emphasis on theory, plus his lucid writing and effective editing, have helped make HCI a success.

– Ben Shneiderman

John M. "Jack" Carroll is widely regarded as one of the founding fathers of HCI, having published some of the earliest scholarship on the subject that in turn established HCI as a distinct sub-discipline of computer science.

Carroll is perhaps best known for being the father of the minimalist school of computer instruction design. Minimalist theory embraces user error as a teaching opportunity, while reducing the extraneous noise that can confuse the user. By reducing the noise, the user-trainees can more effectively focus on the information supporting the decision they are making, which in turn allows for more effective instruction.

Jack Carroll (on left) with Thomas Malone at the ACM CHI Conference on Human Factors in Computing Systems in Toronto, Canada in 1987.

Carroll is the author or co-author of more than 20 books. He was editor-in-chief of the *ACM*

Transactions on Computer Human Interaction (2003–2009) and currently edits the Morgan & Claypool series on Human-Centered Informatics. He received the ACM CHI Lifetime Achievement Award in 2003 and was elected as a Fellow of AAAS, ACM, IEEE, Human Factors and Ergonomics Society, Psychonomics Society, Society for Technical Communication, and Association for Psychological Science. He received an honorary doctorate in Engineering from Universidad Carlos III de Madrid in 2012.

Jack Carroll (left) with Diane Cerra, Mary Beth Rosson, and Rom Baeker at the ACM CHI Conference on Human Factors in Computing Systems in Seattle, WA in 2000.

Affiliations:

➢ Frymoyer Chair of Information Sciences and Technology (2003–Present), Distinguished Professor of Information Sciences and Technology, Penn State University

➢ Head, Department of Computer Science, Virginia Tech (1994–2003)

➢ IBM Watson Research Center

Links:

➢ Homepage

➢ Wikipedia

ELIZABETH CHURCHILL
UBICOMP PIONEER

Elizabeth Churchill is fiercely engaged in making every moment of life and work special. Her vibrant spirit finds ways of being creative professionally as she cleverly designs user experiences or pursues novel theories. She writes energetically, expressing strong views on design issues, and gives generously to SIGCHI and ACM in making our discipline stronger and more collegial.

– Ben Shneiderman

Elizabeth Churchill is an applied social scientist who has assisted in shaping some of the biggest companies in the world, including Yahoo!, eBay, and Google. With a background in experimental psychology and AI, and a keen passion for Human Factors and Design, she is a key researcher in Design Ethnography and has been responsible for innovative products and user experiences since the late 1990s. Examples include, understanding how people communicate in virtual worlds (she started and co-chaired the Collaborative Virtual Environments conference in the mid-1990s through the early 2000s); designing Embodied Conversational Agents, agents that use human-like gestures and expressions to communicate with people; developing and deploying interactive community digital bulletin boards; and promoting many kinds of informal collaborative tools and social media.

Elizabeth Churchill, Joy Mountford, and Wendy Kellogg at the ACM CHI Conference on Human Factors in Computing Systems in Austin, TX in April 2012.

For companies like eBay and Yahoo!, she has worked on improving recommendation algorithms "under the hood" as well as user experiences. She also collaborated on improving instrumentation to develop better user models. Her work on online politeness led the *San Jose Mercury News* to dub her the "Miss Manners of the Web" in 2010.

Churchill has worked extensively in ubiquitous computing, an area that seeks to break free of the desktop computing model by allowing the machinery to go anywhere, including on laptops, tablets, and mobile phones. Churchill manages research for Material Design, Google's primary design system, and for Flutter and Fuchsia, two innovative areas of exploration and innovation at Google.

Allison Druin, Elizabeth Churchill, and Jennifer Preece at the ACM CHI Conference on Human Factors in Computing Systems in Austin, TX, May 5-10, 2012.

Churchill was made an ACM CHI Academy Fellow in 2016, and received an honorary doctorate at University of Sussex, UK in 2018. She served as ACM SIGCHI Vice President and is ACM Vice President (2018-2019).

Affiliations:

> ➤ Director of User Experience, Google (2014–Present)

> ➤ Director, Human Computer Interaction, eBay Research Labs (2012–2014)

> ➤ Principal Research Scientist, Yahoo! Research (2006–2012)

Links:

> ➤ Homepage

> ➤ Wikipedia

JOËLLE COUTAZ
HCI SOFTWARE EXPERT AND TRAILBLAZER IN FRANCE

*Joëlle Coutaz is widely recognized for her thoughtful lead-
ership for CHI in France and for establishing a prominent
research lab at the University of Grenoble. She had impact
through her international efforts to promote the notion of
"plasticity" in user interfaces so as to accommodate diverse user
needs and technology platforms. I was impressed during my
visit to her lab in Grenoble and appreciated the strong community she has built.*

– Ben Shneiderman

Joëlle Coutaz, whose pioneering research helped shape the field of HCI in France, first touched a
computer mouse at Carnegie Mellon University (CMU) in 1982. Coutaz returned to CMU as a
scientific visitor and enjoyed access to personal workstations, which did not yet exist in France. Out
of curiosity, she attended the 1983 ACM CHI Conference on Human Factors in Computing Systems in Boston, MA. The conference inspired Coutaz to set aside her previous research in operating
systems and pursue the software aspects of HCI.

In 1987, Coutaz authored the presentation-abstraction-control (PAC) model, a software
architectural pattern that divides an interactive system into three types of components: the presentation, which formats the audio/visual presentation of data; the abstraction, which retrieves and
processes data; and the control, which facilitates the flow of control and communication between
the other two components.

Coutaz later contributed to the ESPRIT BRA/LTR project AMODEUS (1989-1995), the
first project to promote a multidisciplinary approach to HCI. She also founded the Ingénierie de
l'Interaction Homme-Machine (an HCI research group) at the Laboratory of Informatics of Grenoble in 1990 and served as its head until 2010.

Coutaz was elected to the SIGCHI Academy in 2007. The following year, she coordinated a
working group on Ambient Intelligence for the French Ministry of Research to develop an interdisciplinary field that would approach societal challenges in novel ways. The International Federation
for Information Processing awarded Coutaz the title IFIP TC13 Pioneer in 2013, recognizing her
"outstanding contributions to the educational, theoretical, technical, commercial aspects of analysis,

design, construction, evaluation and use of interactive systems." In 2013, Coutaz was awarded the Legion of Honor by the Republic of France for her pioneering contributions to HCI.

Jun Rekimoto, Christopher Schmandt, Karen Holtzblatt, Mary Czerwinski, Joëlle Coutaz, and Robert Jacob (left to right) at the ACM CHI Conference on Human Factors in Computing Systems in San Jose, CA, April 28–May 3, 2007.

Affiliations:

➢ Professor Emeritus (2012–Present), Professor (1973–2012), Université de Grenoble-Alpes

➢ Co-Chief Editor, JIPS (*Journal of Interaction Person System*)

➢ Expert, ANR (Agence Nationale de Recherche)

➢ Head of the Ingénierie de l'Interaction Homme-Machine (HCI research group), Laboratory of Informatics of Grenoble (1990–2010)

Links:

➢ Homepage

➢ Wikipedia

MARY CZERWINSKI
PIONEER OF MULTITASKING

In my dozens of encounters with Mary at conferences and Microsoft, she was consistently energetic, informed, and ready to work on fresh ideas. Her tenure in the SIGCHI leadership brought new energy to the group, engaging young researchers and advancing the community. Her public talks draw strong crowds, whom she inspires with her stories of using research methods to shape products. I once challenged an assumption in Mary's work, to which she responded sympathetically, and when we next met she presented a research study with important new results about menu design. She has a remarkable ability to take research ideas and produce theoretical insights plus commercially viable product features.

– Ben Shneiderman

Mary Czerwinski keeps interaction at the forefront of her research, which focuses on how humans work, particularly their ability to multitask, visualize information, and apply it to a variety of devices and programs. To this end, she focused her career on improving designs to maximize effectiveness, minimize interruptions, and improve group awareness, which has in turn garnered her more than 30 U.S. patents. During her lengthy tenure as Research Manager at Microsoft, she pursued advanced research and influenced many products that have benefited millions of customers. Czerwinski served as SIGCHI Executive Vice President from 2003–2006, was elected to the ACM CHI Academy in 2010, and made ACM Fellow in 2015.

Mary Czerwinski (right) raises a glass with Ben Shneiderman, Ebad Banissi, and Robert Spence at the International Conference on Information Visualisation in London, England, UK in July 2001.

Mary Czerwinski and Jim Miller at the ACM CHI Conference on Human Factors in Computing Systems in The Hague, The Netherlands in April 2000.

Affiliation:

➤ Adjunct Faculty, iSchool (2011–Present); Affiliate faculty, Department of Psychology (1996–2009); University of Washington

➤ Editorial Board, *Information Visualization*, (2003–Present)

➤ Executive Vice-President (2003–2006), Communications Vice-President (2001–2002), ACM SIGCHI

➤ Research Manager, Visualization and Interaction Research Group, Microsoft Research (1995–Present)

➤ Research Lead, Software Human Factors Design and Test, Compaq Computer Corporation (1990–1995)

Links

➤ Microsoft Research Biography

➤ Washington Post article on Czerwinski's work, published January 2014

CLARISSE DE SOUZA
SEMIOTIC THEORIST

Clarisse worked for decades to teach a younger generation of Brazilian students, turning out doctoral students who spread out around Brazilian universities, helping to make Brazil a leading country in HCI research. Her creative approach of applying semiotics to HCI design broadened our field and opened up new avenues for design thinking. One of the great things about Brazilian researchers is that they know how to party and enjoy life.

– Ben Shneiderman

Clarisse de Souza is the developer of Semiotic Engineering—widely regarded as the first comprehensive theory of semiotics in HCI—a metacommunications theory in which the designers and the users take part in a conversation about the user's needs through the medium of the computer. The goal is to help the designer achieve a better system by guiding the user to describe not only the choices being made, but the reasons why. De Souza has published three books on the subject.

Clarisse de Souza and her brother, Cid Carvalho de Souza, Professor at the Computing Institute of the University of Campinas, at the ACM CHI Conference on Human Factors in Computing Systems in Paris, France in April 2013.

Throughout her career, de Souza has been instrumental in helping to build the HCI community in Brazil, including supervising many budding scholars in the field. Her continuing research is focused on how to express qualitative information, such as beliefs and cultural values, both to and through computers. She was elected to the ACM CHI Academy in 2013.

De Souza, Simon Plumtree, and Jennifer Preece at the ACM CHI Conference on Human Factors in Computing Systems in Seattle, WA, March 30 – April 5, 2001.

Affiliations:

➤ Professor, Department of Informatics, Pontifical Catholic University-Rio (2002–Present)

➤ Assistant Professor (1988–2006), Visiting Professor (1987–1988), Department of Informatics, Pontifical Catholic University-Rio

➤ Head of the Natural Language Database Querying Systems Design Group, EMBRATEL (1982–1988)

Links:

➤ Homepage

SUSAN DRAY
INTERNATIONAL INNOVATOR

Susan's early involvement with SIGCHI researchers and business professionals did much to solidify our emerging discipline. She worked hard for SIGCHI, earning the Lifetime Service Award, and then being elected to the CHI Academy. In recent years, she has become a leader for efforts to apply HCI thinking for international development, ultimately becoming a Fulbright Fellow in Panama to teach HCI.

– Ben Shneiderman

Susan Dray brings a unique background as a psychologist and ethnographer to her work in the field of HCI . She has studied money transfer systems in the African Bush and pay-as-you-go computing in Russia and India, and she helped develop an HCI curriculum in Panama. As the founder and president of Dray and Associates, she consults for the biggest names in multinational corporations and the smallest startups. Along the way, she has mentored dozens of students, which she describes as the accomplishment in which she takes the most pride.

Susan Dray (center) with Nicole Yankelovich and Floris Van Nes at the ACM CHI Conference on Human Factors in Computing Systems in Boston, MA in April 1994.

Dray also developed one of the first usability labs outside of the computer industry during her time with American Express. Having seen a need, she achieved her novel idea by giving a copy of Don Norman's *The Psychology of Everyday Things* to every American Express company executive and waiting until they had all read it before pitching the idea.

Susan Dray and Raoul Smith at the ACM CHI Conference on Human Factors in Computing Systems in Boston, MA in April 1994.

Dray received the CHI Lifetime Service Award in 2006, was elected to the CHI Academy in 2014, was honored with the CHI Lifetime Achievement in Practice Award in 2015, and elected an ACM Fellow in 2017. Outside ACM she was made Human Factors and Ergonomics Society (HFES) Fellow and received the UXPA Lifetime Achievement Award in 2016.

Affiliations:

➤ Fulbright Scholar and Visiting Professor, Universidad Technologica de Panama (2014)

➤ Dray and Associates Inc. (1993–Present)

➤ Director, Human Factors, American Express Financial Advisors (formerly IDS) (1988–1993)

Links:

➤ ACM CHI Lifetime Achievement in Practice Award Biography 2015

ALLISON DRUIN
CHAMPION OF CHILDREN'S COMPUTING

Allison arrived on campus bringing the energy of her already-famous CHI-Kids events at the CHI conferences to the University of Maryland's Human-Computer Interaction Lab. She established the year-long KidsTeam activities, which initiated the ideas of "children as our design partners" and intergenerational teams. Allison gained further respect for HCI research on children by launching the Interaction Design for Children Conference. One of my most satisfying professional accomplishments was attracting Allison and Ben Bederson to our campus. Allison became HCIL Director in 2006.

— Ben Shneiderman

Allison Druin is known for being a futurist and a leading HCI researcher working with children. Druin's professional focus on children began with the development of Noobie, an interactive computer terminal that breaks away from traditional ideas of HCI by coming in the form of a massive bird-like creature that enables kids to build their own digital creatures through interfacing with its parts and incorporated monitor—all done while sitting in Noobie's lap.

During her tenure as the director of the University of Maryland's HCI Lab, she inaugurated an intergenerational development team that brought children aged 7–11 into the interface design process. She also built the International Children's Digital Library, in conjunction with Ben Bederson, and she is a past Chief Futurist for University of Maryland's Division of Research.

Druin currently leads, mentors, and supports the research and strategic partnerships at Pratt Institute. The research spans from advanced interactive materials for the fashion future to understanding the impact of a food barge on food deserts in New York City.

She was elected to the ACM CHI Academy in 2016 and as an ACM Fellow in 2017. She was appointed by the SICHI EC to be the organization's first Adjunct Chair for Inclusion in 2018.

Allison Druin and young colleagues testing the International Children's Digital Library launch at the Library of Congress in Washington, DC on November 20, 2002.

Affiliations:

➢ Associate Provost for Research and Strategic Partnerships, Pratt Institute (2017–Present)

➢ Special Advisor for National Digital Strategy, National Park Service, (2015–2017)

➢ Co-Director, University of Maryland Future of Information Alliance (2013–2017)

➢ Chief Futurist, Division of Research (2013–2015); Director, Human-Computer Interaction Lab (2006–2011); Professor, College of Information Studies (1998–2017); University of Maryland

Links:

➢ Homepage

➢ ACM CHI Social Impact Award 2012—Biography

SUSAN DUMAIS
ELANGUAGE INNOVATOR

My long history of encounters with Sue Dumais go back to her capable young days as a junior research psychologist working with Tom Landauer to her senior research leadership role at Microsoft. Her deep and broad knowledge of the HCI and information retrieval research literature makes her a great source in any discussion. Her clear thinking about work and about her life choices make for satisfying dinner conversations.

– Ben Shneiderman

Susan Dumais and her colleagues at Bellcore (now Telcordia) developed the Latent Semantic Indexing (LSI) system to address the vocabulary mismatch problem, which arises when there is a discrepancy between the words a searcher and the creator of an information item respectively use to describe the same thing. This situation is highlighted by the limited success of Boolean operators in sometimes amusing ways. Dumais' work in LSI solved this problem by quantifying the contextual similarities of words in various texts and then extrapolating out to gauge the content of a particular work by analyzing the combined context of the words in it.

Dan Russell, Marti Hearst, Ben Shneiderman, Susan Dumais, and Ed Chi (left to right) at the ACM CHI Conference on Human Factors in Computing Systems in Paris, France, April 27 – May 2, 2013.

At Microsoft, Susan worked closely with several product groups to improve search systems and experiences used by millions of people every day, from desktop search in Windows to personalization in web search. Much of this research highlights how search systems can be improved by understanding, representing, and using contextual signals to improve results. In all of her research, Susan takes an interdisciplinary and user-centered perspective in designing information systems and experiences. Her contributions have helped build bridges between the HCI, information retrieval, and data science communities.

Justine Cassell, Susan Dumais, Wendy Kellogg, and Ben Shneiderman at the ACM CHI Conference on Human Factors in Computing Systems in Seattle, WA on April 4, 2001.

Dumais received the ACM SIGIR Salton Award for Lifetime Achievement in 2009 and the ACM Athena Lecturer Award in 2014. She was elected to the CHI Academy in 2005, as an ACM Fellow in 2006, as a Member of the National Academy of Engineering in 2009, and as a Member of the American Academy of Arts and Sciences in 2015.

Affiliations:

➤ Adjunct Professor, University of Washington (2002–Present)

➤ Technical Fellow and Deputy Managing Director, Microsoft Research Lab, (1997–Present)

➤ Director, Bell Communications Research (Bellcore, now Telcordia) (1984–1997)

Links:

➤ Homepage

➤ Wikipedia

DOUG ENGELBART
INVENTOR OF THE MOUSE AND VIDEO CONFERENCING

Doug Engelbart was an early hero who promoted intelligence augmentation (IA) in place of AI. His efforts to help knowledge workers be more effective led to his historic demonstration in 1968, in which he showed a large wooden mouse for pointing, chord keyboard for text entry, file sharing, and collaborative methods such as video conferencing. We met in 1985, but my first discussions with him were at the 1987 Hypertext conference. My 1998 encounter with Doug, when he received the first Lifetime Achievement Award at the ACM SIGCHI Conference, was especially moving. He tearfully told me that he greatly appreciated the recognition, which helped soothe the pain he felt because his human-centered work had been fiercely opposed by those who advocated machine-centered models. His gentle soft-spoken style and personal vulnerability was very different from most other HCI Pioneers. The happy outcome was that as his work became widely known; he received worldwide acclaim.

– Ben Shneiderman

Doug Engelbart's most prominent contribution to the field of HCIn was the invention of the computer mouse, for which he held the original patent.

Doug Engelbart (right) and Ben Shneiderman at the CHI Conference on Human Factors in Computing Symposium in Los Angeles, CA on April 18, 1998.

Engelbart rose to prominence in the 1960s, when he gave what has become known as the "Mother of all Demos" at the

1968 Fall Joint Computer Conference in San Francisco, CA. During this presentation, Engelbart demonstrated the oN-Line System (NLS), which featured many of the elements prevalent in modern computing, including the use of a mouse and keyboard for efficient navigation and input, video-conferencing, multiple windows, and collaborative work functions. Engelbart's vision was to shift the focus from the computer to the user, making the screen, keyboard, and mouse as important as the circuits and storage.

His visionary designs in the 1960s played a key role in the emergence of the personal computer and the rise of user interface research. Engelbart was especially interested in collaborative work and created the Bootstrap Institute in his later career to spearhead efforts to do better work through increasing the "collective IQ," an idea that has come to fruition through the ready availability of services such as Google's shared drives and Web 2.0.

Doug Engelbart with colleagues at the Hypertext 1989 Conference in Pittsburgh, PA.

Affiliations:

➢ Co-Founder, Douglas Engelbart (Bootstrap) Institute (1988–2013)

➢ McDonnell Douglas (1984–1989)

➢ Tymshare (1977–1984)

Links:

➢ Wikipedia

➢ The Doug Engelbart Institute

STEVEN FEINER
AUGMENTING REALITY

Steve's deep strengths in software engineering and graphics led him to a path of valuable contributions in augmented reality and algorithms for HCI. I enjoyed my visits to his lab at Columbia University, where he and his students were always showing something new and interesting.

– Ben Shneiderman

Steven Feiner is a pioneer in the world of Augmented Reality (AR). Unlike virtual reality, which replaces the real world with a virtual one, Augmented Reality integrates the two. Feiner published some of the first scholarly papers on AR, including his work on an AR window manager in 1991 and the KARMA knowledge-based AR maintenance assistant in 1992–1993.

Feiner and Thea Turner at INTERCHI, Amsterdam, The Netherlands, April 24-29, 1993.

For more than 20 years, Feiner's work has pioneered augmented reality systems to bring this technology to numerous domains and take AR into the field for the first time. With fellow pioneers

James Foley and Andy Van Dam, Feiner is the co-author of the benchmark *Computer Graphics: Principles and Practice* textbook.

Feiner has also conducted research in a multitude of related areas, including 3D user interfaces, wearable computing, and computer games. Feiner was inducted into the SIGCHI Academy in 2011 and made a Fellow of the IEEE in 2018. He received the ACM UIST 2010 Lasting Impact Award, IEEE Visualization and Graphics Technical Committee 2014 Virtual Reality Career Award, IEEE International Symposium on Mixed and Augmented Reality 2017 Career Impact Award, and the International Symposium on Wearable Computers 2017 Early Innovator Award.

Brad Myers presenting Steven Feiner with the award commemorating Feiner's election to the CHI Academy at the ACM CHI Conference on Human Factors in Computing Systems in Vancouver, British Columbia, Canada, May 7–12, 2011.

Affiliations:

➢ Lead Advisor, Meta (2012–Present)

➢ Professor, Computer Science, Columbia University (1985–Present)

Links:

➢ Homepage

➢ Wikipedia

GERHARD FISCHER
DISCIPLINE BRIDGER

Gerhard's thoughtful writings on HCI, collaboration, education, and other topics made me think in fresh ways and learn about new sources. I also value his remarkable skiing ability and style, gained from his youthful experience of being a ski instructor. Skiing with Gerhard made me a better skier, talking with Gerhard made me a better researcher.

– Ben Shneiderman

Gerhard Fischer's work has, according to SIGCHI, "played a crucial role as an integrator of and mediator between HCI and a spectrum of related fields: AI, Software Engineering, Participatory Design, Computer Supported Collaborative Learning, and CSCW. His work has extended the boundaries of our field."

Jennifer Preece and Gerhard Fischer at a Masterclass and Symposium hosted at the University of Canterbury in Christchurch, New Zealand on March 20, 2003.

In addition to his bridge-building, Fischer has also conducted extensive research in education (lifelong learning, self-directed learning, and organizational learning), and cognitive science (mental models and learning environments).

Fischer was elected to the SIGCHI Academy in 2007.

Fischer at the National Science Foundation Creativity Conference at the University of Colorado on November 3, 2006.

Affiliations:

- ➢ Professor, Computer Science Department, University of Colorado—Boulder and Fellow of the Institute of Cognitive Science (1984–2012), Emeritus Professor (2012–Present)

- ➢ Director, Center for LifeLong Learning and Design, University of Colorado—Boulder (1994–Present)

Links:

- ➢ Homepage
- ➢ Wikipedia

JAMES FOLEY
GRAPHICS HCI PIONEER

Jim's early book Computer Graphics: Principles and Practice *with Andy Van Dam is one of the true classics that guided many young researchers to understand the user interface aspects of graphics. Jim was an early partner in shaping the Software Psychology Society (1976-1996) that promoted HCI in the Washington, DC area and nationally. Jim's been a trusted and valued colleague, who gave generously to his students and to professional groups, such as the Computing Research Association, while always expanding his elaborate model train installation.*

– Ben Shneiderman

James D. Foley is a leading expert in computer graphics. Along with fellow pioneer Andy van Dam, and later with Steven Feiner and John Hughes, Foley co-authored several fundamental texts on computer graphics. In 1991, he founded Georgia Tech's GVU Center (previously the Graphics, Visualization and Usability Center), which in five years became the nation's leading graduate research institute in the fields of HCI, information visualization, mixed/augmented reality, wearable computing, educational technologies, online communities, and computer graphics.

James Foley (left) and Robert Ball experimenting with exhibits at the IEEE Symposium on Information Visualization (InfoVis) in Baltimore, MD on November 1, 2006.

Foley was elected to the SIGCHI Academy in 2001 and was the recipient of the Lifetime Achievement Award in 2007. He is a Fellow of AAAS, ACM, and IEEE, as well as a member of the National Academy of Engineering. Foley received the ACM SIGGRAPH Steven Anson Coons Award for Outstanding Creative Contributions to Computer Graphics in 1997.

Foley (far right) upon receiving his SIGCHI Lifetime Achievement Award with the members of the SIGCHI Academy Class of 2007 at the ACM CHI Conference on Human Factors in Computing Systems in San Jose, CA on May 13, 2007.

Affiliations:

> Professor, Stephen Fleming Chair in Telecommunications, School of Interactive Computing, Georgia Institute of Technology (2000–Present)

> Director MS-HCI, Georgia Tech (2011–2014)

> Executive Director later CEO, Yamacraw Economic Development Initiative (1999–2000)

> President, Mitsubishi Information Technology America (1997–1999)

Links:

> Homepage

> Wikipedia

SAUL GREENBERG
UBIQUITOUS COMPUTING EXPERT

Saul Greenberg's early and consistent devotion to building HCI excellence is clear in his work on physical devices, collaboration, tool kits for rapid prototyping, and evaluation methods. The diversity of his work is impressive, combining diligent data collection and innovative implementations all guided by appropriate theories. I've always enjoyed my times talking with Saul, especially skiing behind him to admire his graceful style. His cheerful can-do personality is appealing. Saul is one of those exceptional people who I wish I could spend more time with.

– Ben Shneiderman

Saul Greenberg is a computer scientist specializing in situated interaction—how people incorporate computer technology in their daily lives. His research has provided better understanding of how computer technology fits within people's physical environment and how people use such technology for both work and social interaction.

At the University of Calgary, the work by Greenberg and his talented crew typifies the cross-discipline aspects of HCI, computer-supported cooperative work, and ubiquitous computing. He and his team are well known for their development of:

- toolkits enabling rapid prototyping of groupware and ubiquitous appliances;

- innovative and seminal system designs based on observations of social phenomenon;

- support teams of people using technology for their many styles of collaboration, including across time, over distance, and for casual or formal interactions;

- articulation of design-oriented social science theories; and

- refinement of evaluation methods.

Greenberg has written and edited several books and published many articles. Researchers and educators in the field benefit from Greenberg's commitment to ensuring that his tools, systems, and educational materials are readily available. In addition to his academic work, Greenberg has consulted for various companies as an expert witness in matters involving patent infringement.

Saul Greenberg with two former graduate students, Michael Rounding (center) and Michael Boyle (right), at the ACM Conference on Computer-Supported Cooperative Work (CSCW) in Philadelphia, PA on December 2, 2000. Rounding and Boyle are now seasoned HCI practitioners.

Greenberg was elected to the prestigious ACM CHI Academy in April 2005 and was inducted as an ACM Fellow in 2013 for his contributions to computer supported cooperative work and ubiquitous computing. He received the Canadian Human Computer Communications Society Achievement Award in May 2007, the ACM UIST Lasting Impact award in 2015, and the Canadian Digital Media Pioneer Award in 2018.

Affiliations:

➢ Former Professor in Computer Science, current Emeritus/Faculty Professor, University of Calgary (1991–Present)

➢ President, Greenberg Consulting, Inc.

➢ Adjunct Professor in the Department of Psychology (Calgary), Department of Computer Science (Saskatchewan)

Links:

➢ Homepage

➢ GroupLab Site

HIROSHI ISHII
TANGIBLE REALITY

Hiroshi's energetic smile and intense presentations promoted tangible computing ideas at MIT and beyond. His vibrant demos and videos opened the door to the physicality of user interfaces. I like his enthusiasm and his fresh ideas, and we share an interest in taking photos of our colleagues.

– Ben Shneiderman

Hiroshi Ishii is the creator of the Tangible User Interface (TUI), which allows a user to interact with digital information in non-standard ways. Ishii first described the concept in his paper "Tangible Bits." Moving beyond the ubiquitous keyboard and mouse, TUIs seek to allow the manipulation of digital information through physical modules, making the "bits" more open to direct manipulation and opening a variety of information types to users.

The SIGCHI Academy class of 2006 (from left): George Robertson, Hiroshi Ishii, Jakob Nielsen, Michel Beaudoin-Lafond, Scott Hudson, and Peter Pirolli at the ACM CHI Conference on Human Factors in Computing Systems in Montreal Canada on April 24, 2006.

Ishii's continued research in the area has led to the Radical Atoms, an as yet theoretical successor generation of Tangible Bits that are themselves changeable and, according to the Tangible Media Group, would become "as reconfigurable as pixels on a screen." He received the ACM CHI Lifetime Research Award in 2019.

Hiroshi Ishii with Patrick Baudisch at the ACM CHI Conference on Human Factors in Computing Systems in Paris, France in April 2013.

Affiliations:

➤ Jerome B. Weisner Professor of Media Arts and Sciences, MIT Media Lab (1995–Present)

➤ Visiting Professor, University of Toronto (1993–1994)

➤ Lead Scientist, CSCW Research Group, NTT Human Interface Laboratories (1988–1994)

Links:

➤ Homepage

➤ Wikipedia

ROBERT JACOB
USER INTERFACE SOFTWARE EXPERT

*Rob Jacob has been a reliable and highly competent contrib-
utor to HCI research and in service to the ACM SIGCHI
community. His research helped clarify design principles for
input devices based on integrality and separability, extending
our understanding of direct manipulation principles. His work
on eye tracking showed what was possible for research and explored the possibilities for eye-gaze interaction. Rob was generous in supporting his students and in bringing newcomers to
HCI with his regular tutorials at the CHI conference.*

– Ben Shneiderman

Robert Jacob, a Professor of Computer Science at Tufts University, is a pioneering investigator of
new user interface software and interaction techniques. His research enabled experts in the field of
HCI to apply system design, theoretical analysis, and quantitative measurement to the concurrent
real-world interactions facilitated by contemporary, post-WIMP ("window, icon, menu, pointing
device") interfaces. Jacob's current research group focuses on a new generation of brain-computer
interfaces. While the primary application for brain-computer interaction to date has been for physically disabled users, Jacob and his team aim to develop and evaluate brain measurement as input
for adaptable user interfaces for the larger population.

*Jacob with Batya Friedman
and Jonathan Lazar at the ACM
CHI Conference on Human Factors in
Computing Systems in Austin, TX in
May 2012.*

In the 1990s, Jacob and others in
the field of HCI observed a divergence
from the WIMP or Direct Manipulation
interaction style. As a new generation
of post-WIMP interfaces emerged, Jacob led a research project introducing the notion of reali-

ty-based interaction as a unifying concept to tie together a large subset of the new interaction styles. Although some experts considered the new interaction techniques to be disparate innovations developing on unrelated tracks, reality-based interaction highlighted the ways in which the new interaction styles drew strength from building upon users' pre-existing knowledge of the everyday, non-digital world. This focus on commonalities between the new interaction techniques aided researchers in their efforts to understand, connect, and analyze them.

Jacob is a member of the editorial boards of *ACM TOCHI*, *Human–Computer Interaction*, and the *International Journal of Human–Computer Studies* and has served as chair of ACM CHI, UIST, and TEI conferences. He was elected to the ACM CHI Academy in 2007.

Jacob with Dan Olsen, Scott Hudson, and Brad Myers at the ACM Symposium on User Interface Software and Technology (UIST) in Vancouver, BC, Canada on November 2, 2003.

Affiliations:

➤ Professor of Computer Science (previously Associate, Assistant), Department of Computer Science, Tufts University (1994–Present)

➤ Vice President of ACM SIGCHI (2014–2015, 2001–2006, 1990–1993)

➤ Visiting Lecturer, University College London Interaction Centre (2014)

Links:

➤ Rob Jacob—Tufts University

➤ ACM Fellow 2016

BONNIE JOHN
COGNITIVE MODELING PIONEER

Bonnie John was devoted to computational models of user behavior, particularly the Goals, Operators, Methods, and Selection rules to predict user performance. Her success in cases of expert users performing routine tasks showed the value of cognitive models. Bonnie did admirable work in shaping our discipline through her participation in numerous technical program committees and editorial boards. In addition to these contributions, Bonnie will be remembered for her playful side, hearty laugh, and her courageous juggling at the CHI 1994 dance party.

– Ben Shneiderman

Bonnie E. John is an American cognitive psychologist who studies HCI, predictive human performance modeling, and the relationship between usability and software architecture. She was a founding member of the Human-Computer Interaction Institute at Carnegie Mellon University, a research Staff Member at IBM's Thomas J. Watson Research Center, and the Director of Computation and Innovation at The Cooper Union. She is currently a UX designer at Bloomberg L.P., and she has published more than 100 technical papers in the area of HCI.

Bonnie John with Thomas Landauer at the ACM CHI Conference on Human Factors in Computing Systems in Portland, OR, April 2-7, 2005.

John focuses on cognitive modeling, working within a unified theory of cognition to develop models of human performance that produce quantitative predictions of performance with less effort than prototyping and user testing. She researches techniques to improve the design of computer systems, particularly their usefulness and usability. She has investigated the effectiveness and usability of several HCI techniques, including think-aloud usability studies, Cognitive Walk-through, and GOM. John has produced new techniques for bringing usability concerns to the design process, such as CPM-GOMS and Usability-Supporting Architectural patterns. Her team at Carnegie Mellon University developed CogTool, an open-source tool to support Keystroke-Level Model analysis.

Bonnie John with Toni Robertson at the HCI International Conference in Crete, Greece, June 22-27, 2003.

She directed the Masters in HCI Program in Human–Computer Interaction at Carnegie Mellon University from 1997 to 2009 and was a founding Associate Editor for *ACM Transactions on Computer Human Interaction* (TOCHI). She regularly serves on the ACM SIGCHI conference program committee and was elected to the CHI Academy in 2005. John was a Research Staff Member at IBM's Thomas J. Watson Research Center from December 2010–December 2014. She returned to her alma mater, The Cooper Union, as the Director of Computation and Innovation in December 2014. In July 2015, she joined Bloomberg's UX design team, to focus primarily on discoverability of new functionality on the Bloomberg Terminal.

Affiliations:

➢ Faculty at Carnegie Mellon University, School of Computer Science, Department of Psychology and Human-Computer Interaction Institute (1989–1996)

➢ Consultant for Microsoft, Software Engineering Institute, CarnegieWorks, American Robot Corp., AT&T, and NYNEX.

Links:

➢ Wikipedia

➢ Carnegie Mellon Homepage

JEFF JOHNSON
USABILITY WIZARD

Jeff's early devotion to ethical issues in computing was apparent in his conference talks and professional activism. I respected and learned from his strong statements on social issues. He succeeded as a consultant and author, repeatedly turning out influential books, such as his series of books on GUI Bloopers *and* Web Bloopers. *His bold views are in* Designing with the Mind in Mind: Simple Guide to Understanding User Interface Design Guidelines.

– Ben Shneiderman

Jeff Johnson is a prolific author and consultant, who provides advanced product usability consulting to major corporations and brings his experience to the masses through his books on achieving good design. His firm, UI Wizards Inc. provides training to help non-technical executives learn what they need to know to make good decisions and work constructively with technical staff.

Johnson and Blaise Liffick at the ACM CHI Conference on Human Factors in Computing Systems in Atlanta, GA, March 22-27, 1997.

Jeff Johnson at the ACM CHI Conference on Human Factors in Computing Systems in Ft. Lauderdale, FL on April 9, 2003.

Johnson has twice been named an Erskine Fellow to the Computer Science and Software Engineering Department at the University of Canterbury, New Zealand.

He received ACM SIGCHI's Lifetime Achievement in Practice Award in 2016.

Affiliations:

- ➤ Assistant Professor, University of San Francisco (2016–Present)
- ➤ President, UI Wizards Inc. (1996–Present)
- ➤ Human Interface Engineer, Sun Microsystems (1993–1996)
- ➤ Technical Staff, Hewlett-Packard Laboratories (1988–1993)

Links:

- ➤ Homepage
- ➤ USF Homepage

ALAN KAY
INVENTOR OF THE LAPTOP

Kay's early vision of the Dynabook suggested a book-sized portable computer, which was a wild idea in the days of room-sized computers, but he proved to be right. He also contributed software technology and user interface concepts to realize this vision. His playful style and sharp insights made his talks worth listening to, and his devotion to computers that kids could use was admirable.

– Ben Shneiderman

Alan Kay is one of the earliest pioneers in personal computing, overlapping-window interface, modern object-oriented programming, and the concept of the laptop computer. His quip that "The best way to predict the future is to invent it" is widely repeated. He likes to say that no one owes more to his research community than he does.

Kay was one of the founding researchers of the Xerox Palo Alto Research Center (PARC), where he led the group that developed the overlapping window and icon graphical user interface and the Smalltalk object-oriented language, and which participated in the development of the modern graphical networked personal computer and WYSIWYG desktop publishing.

Kay and Randy Trigg (right) speak at the ACM CHI Conference on Human Factors in Computing in April 1986 in Boston, MA.

Kay is perhaps best known for his Dynabook concept—a vision of a portable device combining hardware, software, and programming tools to offer the ultimate creative suite for children of all ages. This vision, conceptualized in the 1970s, prefigured the modern laptop computer.

His interest in children and education inspired him to establish Viewpoints Research Institute, a non-profit organization dedicated to improve "powerful ideas education" for children and to advance systems research and personal computing. Throughout his career, Kay has demonstrated his commitment to transforming the computer into a dynamic personal medium supporting creative thought.

Kay's long list of honors include the ACM Turing Award in 2003, the Kyoto Prize in 2004, the U. S. National Academy of Engineering Draper Prize (with Butler Lampson, Chuck Thacker, and Bob Taylor), ACM Software Systems Award (with Dan Ingalls and Adele Goldberg), and numerous honorary doctorates. He is a Fellow of the American Academy of Arts and Sciences, National Academy of Engineering, Royal Society of Arts, Computer History Museum, ACM, and the Hasso Plattner Institute.

Kay talks with Marvin Minsky at the International Conference for Interaction Design and Children hosted in June 2004 at the University of Maryland, College Park.

Affiliations:

➤ Co-Founder and President, Viewpoints Research Institute (2001–Present)

➤ Advisory Board Member, TTI/Vanguard (Present)

➤ Adjunct Professor, University of California, Los Angeles (Present)

Links:

➤ Wikipedia

➤ Encyclopaedia Britannica

WENDY KELLOGG
COMPUTER-MEDIATED COMMUNICATION EXPERT

Wendy's social psychology skills were evident in her research and the memorable party when she ran the CHI 1994 conference. Her smiling disposition and energetic commitment made her a strong leader and a natural in founding the IBM Social Computing Group in 1998. The Group helped raise interest in collaborative technologies. Wendy has continued her foundational work in editing the 2014 book Ways of Knowing in HCI *with Judy Olson. And yes, she loves to play golf.*

– Ben Shneiderman

Wendy A. Kellogg is a cognitive psychologist specializing in the design and study of systems to support computer-mediated communication (CMC) in groups and organizations. Throughout her career, she has worked in the areas of social computing, computer-supported cooperative work, and HCI. Kellogg has championed a blend of qualitative and quantitative approaches in her work through the artifact-theory cycle, in a process of design-led research.

Kellogg at the ACM CHI Conference on Human Factors in Computing Systems in New Orleans, LA in April 1991.

A founder of the field of social computing, Kellogg formed the first research group targeting social computing in 1998. The Social Computing Group at IBM's T.J. Watson Research Center concentrated its studies in several areas, originally including computer-mediated communication, social proxies, the design of social software, and enhanced audio conferencing. In its later work, the team addressed interaction in virtual worlds, mobile applications for the next billion users, and patient engagement in medical fields. Kellogg and her colleague Thomas Erickson proposed the term "social translucence" to describe "digital systems that support coherent behavior by making participants and their activities visible to one another." Social translucence is a conceptual framework for designing visual and other structural elements to stimulate online participation, facilitate collaboration, and enable navigation, particularly in online communities and social networking sites.

Kellogg with Elizabeth Churchill (left) and Joy Mountford (center) at the ACM CHI Conference on Human Factors in Computing Systems in Austin, TX in May 2012.

In its 14 years, the Social Computing Group generated more than 150 publications and 36 patents and received significant recognition, including two Best Paper awards from ACM SIGCHI's CHI and CSCW conferences and Outstanding Innovation awards from IBM in 2005 and 2011. Kellogg was elected to the ACM CHI Academy in 2008.

Affiliations:

➢ Research Staff Member, IBM Emeritus (2014–Present)

➢ Social Computing and Cognitive Systems Research, IBM TJ Watson Research Center (2013–2014)

➢ Manager, Social Computing, IBM T.J. Watson Research Center (1998–2013)

Links:

➢ Wikipedia

➢ LinkedIn

SARA KIESLER
PIONEER OF COLLABORATIVE WORK

One of the sharpest analytic minds anywhere. When Sara speaks, I listen carefully because she makes vital distinctions, documented by empirical evidence, and directed toward making an important point. Her devotion to rigorous experimentation gives her a compelling authority when she speaks. I admire her style.

– Ben Shneiderman

Sara Kiesler is a psychologist by education, but has worked extensively to understand how interactions with computers change how humans interact with one another. She is the co-author of *Connections* (with Lee Sproull), which examines how e-mail changes workplaces—some of the first research done on the topic. The work documented in *Connections* continues with studies of personality portrayal and anonymity online.

Sara Kiesler, Ben Shneiderman, Lynn Streeter, and Byron Reeves (left to right) at the ACM CHI Conference on Human Factors in Computing Systems in Denver, CO in May 1995.

Currently, Kiesler is working on collaborative research examining the pros and cons of complex and multidisciplinary projects and groups, data analysis patterns in intelligence analysts, and developing "service delivery frameworks" for human-robot interactions. Kiesler was elected to the CHI Academy in 2002, awarded the SIGCHI Lifetime Achievement Award in 2009, and named an ACM Fellow in 2010. In 2018, she was elected as a Fellow of the American Academy of Arts and Sciences and given the Human Robot Interaction Lifetime Service Award. Since 2016, Kiesler has been a Program Director at the Division of Social and Economic Sciences in the U. S. National Science Foundation. She was elected to the National Academy of Engineering in 2019.

Sara Kiesler with Bonnie John at the ACM CHI Conference on Human Factors in Computing Systems in Atlanta, GA in April 2010.

Affiliations:

- ➢ Hillman Professor of Computer Science and Human-Computer Interaction, Carnegie Mellon University (1999–Present)

- ➢ Interval (1998–1999)

- ➢ Social and Decision Sciences, Carnegie Mellon University (1979–1998)

Links:

- ➢ Homepage

- ➢ Wikipedia

JOSEPH KONSTAN
GROUPLENS PROJECT CONTRIBUTOR

I've followed Joe Konstan's work from the time of his Ph.D. degree at the University of California-Berkeley in 1993. He manifests the focused style and thoughtful competence that I like to see in colleagues. He did great research on online communities—developing a successful collaborative filtering company—authored several patents, was involved in innovative teaching projects, and has an active service record on campus and professionally. During this time as SIGCHI Chair, he helped advance our discipline and build a stronger community.

– Ben Shneiderman

Joseph "Joe" A. Konstan is a Professor of Computer Science and Engineering at the University of Minnesota. His research spans a variety of HCI issues related to filtering, comprehending, organizing, and automating large and complex data sets. One of Konstan's most notable contributions is his ongoing work with GroupLens, a research lab at the University of Minnesota, Twin Cities, specializing in recommender systems, online communities, mobile and ubiquitous technologies, digital libraries, and local geographic information systems. Konstan has also collaborated with partners across disciplines to improve theoretical and empirical understanding of online Q&A sites and to develop persuasive computing applications focusing on altering behaviors to reduce AIDS risk among high-risk individuals.

Joe Konstan with GroupLens lab colleagues John Riedl and Loren Terveen at the NSF Workshop on Social-Computational Systems at the University of Minnesota in Minneapolis, MN in 2011.

The GroupLens lab was one of the first to study automated recommender systems through its development of the "GroupLens" recommender, which functions much like the system Amazon.com uses to recommend purchases to specific users. Konstan joined the GroupLens recommender system project in 1995 and has since worked with the lab's research team to explore technology for creating recommendations and identify how best to present those recommendations so that users find them useful. In recent years, Konstan's focus has shifted to the concept of online communities, particularly how people participate in those communities and how to design communities to elicit participation.

Joe Konstan with Ben Shneiderman at the ACM CHI Conference on Human Factors in Computing Systems in Seattle, WA, March 31—April 5, 2001.

Konstan has chaired or co-chaired several ACM conferences and served as president of ACM SIGCHI from 2003–2006. He was elected as a Fellow of the CHI Academy, ACM, IEEE, and AAAS. He received two prestigious awards: the 2010 ACM Software System Award for the GroupLens Collaborative Filtering Recommender Systems and the 2016 World Wide Web Conference's Seoul Test of Time Award.

Affiliations:

➤ Professor (2005–Present), Associate Professor (1999–2005), Assistant Professor (1993–1999), University of Minnesota

➤ Consulting Scientist, Net Perceptions, Inc. (1996–2000)

Links:

➤ Homepage

➤ GroupLens

ROBERT KRAUT
ONLINE COMMUNITIES GURU

Bob's deep knowledge of social psychology and his strong analytic mind always won my respect and attention. His cleverly designed experiments teased out what works and what doesn't for small collaborations and large communities. His book Building Successful Online Communities: Evidence-based Social Design *(2012, with Paul Resnick) provides clear advice for community designers and researchers. Bob is one of the people with whom I wish I had been able to spend more time.*

– Ben Shneiderman

Robert Kraut is a social psychologist who dedicated his career to research and education on human communication and the impact of computing. His five major research areas include online communities, everyday use of the Internet, collaboration in small work groups, technology and conversation, and computers in organizations. Kraut teaches courses in these areas as a Herbert A. Simon Professor of Human-Computer Interaction at the Human-Computer Interaction Institute at Carnegie Mellon University. He was previously a professor at Cornell, Princeton, and the University of Pennsylvania.

During his early academic career, Kraut conducted basic experiments in nonverbal communication that experts continue to cite today. While working with Bellcore, Kraut studied informal group communication in the workplace and established far-reaching methodologies for studying collaboration. Kraut joined the faculty at Carnegie Mellon University in 1993. As the Internet rapidly expanded in the mid-1990s, Kraut initiated a program of studies on the impact of the Internet in the home on the well-being of its users. His longitudinal studies followed new users over months and years. Kraut's systematic scientific approach to observing social effects transformed the methodology for investigating social phenomena and continues to influence the way people both in the field of HCI and outside the field think about the social impact of technology.

Kraut's most recent research has focused on the analysis and design of online communities, including Facebook, health-supported communities, guilds in multi-player games, and Wikipedia. Facebook brought Kraut in as visiting faculty in 2013.

Robert Kraut with GuSalama, Brad Myers, and Jonathan Lazar (left to right) at CMU in Pittsburgh, PA in November 2005.

Kraut was elected to the CHI Academy in 2003 for "cumulative contirbutions to the field, influence on the work of others, and development of new research directions." He is a fellow of both the Association for Psychological Science and the Association of Computing Machinery (ACM). Kraut received ACM SIGCHI's Lifetime Achievement in Research Award in 2016.

Affiliations:

➢ Herbert A. Simon Professor Emeritus (2018–Present), Herbert A. Simon Professor of Human Computer Interaction, School of Computer Science and Tepper School of Business (2000–2018), Professor, Social Psychology and Human Computer Interaction (1993–2000) Carnegie Mellon University

➢ Member, Computer Science and Telecommunications Board, National Research Council (2010–Present)

➢ Director, Interpersonal Communications Research Program, Bell Communications Research (1987–1993)

Links:

➢ Homepage

➢ Wikipedia

JAMES LANDAY
HCI COMMUNITY BUILDER

I've followed James Landay's work since his grad student days at Carnegie Mellon University, where he worked with Brad Myers on sketching interfaces. Even then, Landay was impressive in his technical abilities and capacity to focus on a problem and produce compelling results presented in solid publications. Landay has an impressive professional career working with companies (Intel, Microsoft, etc.), attracting and nurturing terrific talent, and then pushing teams of students to produce great results. Some find Jim to be a tough guy, but he's always well-intentioned and on the right side of issues I care about, such as sustainable computing.

– Ben Shneiderman

James Landay is a Professor of Computer Science at Stanford University with an outstanding ability to establish communities of HCI researchers with lasting impact on the field. Landay's leadership as director of Intel Labs Seattle from 2003–2006 advanced the laboratory of 20 researchers to prominence as the top laboratory focusing on technologies and applications of ubiquitous computing in the world. At the University of Washington, Landay co-founded the Design. Use. Build. (DUB) Center, an alliance of professors, students, researchers, and industry professionals with shared interest in HCI and design research. Under Landay's leadership, the DUB Center became an internationally acclaimed powerhouse in HCI research. Landay is also the founder and co-director of the World Lab, a cross-cultural research and education collaboration between the University of Washington and Tsinghua University in Beijing.

Landay's research has contributed to areas of ubiquitous computing, automated usability evaluation, web design, and user interface design tools. As a graduate student at Carnegie Mellon University, he began creating tools using sketching to support fluid user interface design and development. Landay was the first to demonstrate the use of sketching in user interface design tools in his pioneering Ph.D. dissertation. In addition to his continued interest in user interface design tools, his current research focuses on technology to support behavior change, demonstrational interfaces, and mobile computing.

Brad Myers presents his former Ph.D. student James Landay with an award recognizing Landay's election to the CHI Academy at the ACM CHI Conference on Human Factors in Computing Systems in Vancouver, BC, Canada in May 2011.

Landay is the co-author of the best-selling web design book *The Design of Sites*. He also co-founded and served as chief scientist at NetRaker, a start-up company in the field that was later acquired by KeyNote Systems. Landay was elected to the CHI Academy in 2011.

Affiliations:

➢ Professor of Computer Science, Stanford University (2014–Present)

➢ Professor of Information Science, Cornell University (2013–2014)

➢ Professor in Computer Science and Engineering (2010–2013), Associate Professor (2003–2010), University of Washington

➢ Director, Intel Research Seattle (2003–2006)

Links:

➢ Homepage

➢ Election to ACM CHI Academy 2011

JARON LANIER
RE-ENFRANCHISING THE INTERNET

Jaron is among the people I cherish because of their brilliant, deep, and independent thinking. He's best known for coining the term "virtual reality," but that's just a fraction of what he has done. My visits with him go back to his New York City days; but he seems to fit in well with the Berkeley hills, where his musical instrument collection fills his home. I love to read his books, eagerly turning the pages, happily agreeing with his fresh way of framing a problem and innovative solutions— sometimes I think he's gone too far, but then I wonder if I haven't gone far enough. His musical presentations and talks are great moments of theater, in which anything can happen.

– Ben Shneiderman

Jaron Lanier is a multi-discipline dynamo. His HCI work has focused on direct interfaces between the human and the computer, including the data glove, virtual reality goggles, and gaming. Following a brief stint at Atari, Lanier founded his own virtual reality research organization, VPL, which later sold its patents to Sun Microsystems. Throughout the late 1990s, Lanier worked on the Internet2 and as a visiting scholar for numerous research institutions.

Jaron Lanier presenting at the ACM CHI Conference on Human Factors in Computing Systems in Seattle, WA in 1990.

Lanier authored *You are Not a Gadget* and *Who Owns the Future* and is openly critical of some Internet2 developments, particularly Wikipedia. He is wary of the distance Wikipedia allows between information and its original author and context. Lanier recognizes the false sense of authority Wikipedia can instill in its readers due to hidden authorship. The work of *Who Owns the Future* serves as a call to re-enfranchise middle-class consumers, who Lanier claims get the least out of the Internet, because they provide their personal information as a commodity but receive little back. Two later books also gained widespread readership: *Dawn of the New Everything: Encounters with Reality and Virtual Reality* (2017) and *Ten Arguments for Deleting Your Social Media Accounts Right Now* (2018).

Lanier is also an accomplished musician and composer. *TIME* magazine named Lanier as one of the most influential thinkers in 2010. He received an honorary doctorate from Franklin and Marshall College in 2012.

Jaron Lanier at home in the Berkeley, CA hills playing harp with his daughter, Lilibell, in October 2010.

Affiliations:

➢ Innovator in Residence, USC Annenberg (2010–Present)

➢ Interdisciplinary Scientist, Microsoft (2009–Present)

➢ Scholar-at-Large, Microsoft Live Labs (2006–2009)

➢ Fellow, International Coimputer Science Institute, Berkley (2004–Present)

➢ Visiting Faculty, Dartmouth College (2001–Present)

Links:

➢ Homepage

➢ Wikipedia

BRENDA LAUREL
VIRTUAL REALITY PIONEER

Brenda Laurel came from a Ph.D. in theater and infused user interface design with fresh thinking that opened up new possibilities, such as performance-based scenarios to guide user experience design. Her own theatricality makes her a compelling public speaker with important messages about how human interaction with and through computers should be designed. Brenda gets credit from me for her admirable advocacy for the needs of young women.

– Ben Shneiderman

Brenda Laurel is a pioneer in the development of virtual reality and one of the earliest advocates in the development of video games for girls. Her unique background in theater gave Laurel fresh perspective on the world of computers and enabled her to show designers and engineers how to consider the people using their products while developing new projects. She began her career at Atari in 1979, first as a software strategist, then as a member of the research staff at the Atari Systems Research Laboratory, where she developed a theory of first-person presence in interactive environments and worked with AI to improve the quality of interactive games.

Abbe Don and Brenda Laurel at the ACM CHI Conference on Human Factors in Computing Systems in Seattle, WA, April 1–5, 1990.

In 1988, she worked with Apple on projects including Vivarium and Guides, a prototype encyclopedia with a storytelling interface. In 1990, she co-founded Telepresence Research, Inc., focusing on virtual reality and remote presence. She co-designed and directed the innovative Placeholder virtual reality project at the Banff Centre for the Arts in 1993.

In 1997, Laurel launched Purple Moon, a software company dedicated to creating games and online communities to engage girls. Purple Moon tailored its game development to the wants and interests of girls. The Starfire Soccer Challenge game, for example, responded to girls' excitement as American women came close to winning the World Cup. Although Purple Moon was acquired by Mattel in 1999 and eventually dissolved, Laurel's work proved to the gaming industry that its audience could be far broader and set the stage for more gender-neutral games, such as the Wii.

Brenda Laurel giving a talk on the Nielsen Tour in London, England on March 3, 2000.

Her career-defining book *Computers as Theatre* (1991, expanded edition in 2014) has influenced many in the User Interface field. She teaches courses in design research, critique, methods for innovation and creativity, and interaction in the polis. Laurel received the Indie-Cade Trailblazer Award in 2015 and the Virtual World Society Nextant Prize in 2017. She was elected to the IxDA Global Board of Directors in 2018 and serves on the Board of the Virtual World Society.

Affiliations:

- Adjunct Professor, University of California at Santa Cruz (July 2013–2015)
- Graduate Program in Design, California College of the Arts (2006–2012)
- Sun Microsystems Laboratories (2005–2006)
- Graduate Media Design Program, Art Center College of Design (1999–2006)
- Principal designer of a curriculum for the New Media Program (1999–2002)
- Purple Moon (1996–1999)

Links:

- Homepage
- Blog post

CLAYTON LEWIS
USABILITY ADVOCATE

My experiences with Clayton go back a long time. He was an early researcher who adapted psychology research methods to the needs of HCI research. Clayton was ready to lead his department, offer bold new ideas, and put himself fully into research and policy making for users with disabilities. Clayton's energetic gestures and distinctive speaking style drew attention from listeners and photographers like me.

– Ben Shneiderman

Clayton Lewis is a Professor of Computer Science and Fellow of the Institute of Cognitive Science at the University of Colorado Boulder. He is renowned for his work in developing methodologies to evaluate user interface design. These methods include the think-aloud protocol, in which researchers observe participants as they talk through their thoughts and actions while completing a set task, and the cognitive walkthrough method, which acknowledges user preference to learn new software through exploration rather than formal training and consequently focuses on evaluating software design for ease of learning.

Lewis with Norman Sondheimer at the ACM CHI Conference on Human Factors in Computing Systems in Boston, MA in December 1983.

In the early 1980s, Lewis led and inspired some of the first HCI projects on user-centered design as the manager of the Human Factors Group at the IBM Watson Research Center. Lewis and his colleagues at IBM Corporate identified usability as a key challenge and research area, which led to the foundation of the IBM User Interface Institute. The usability inspection methods developed by Lewis and his colleagues—including the think-aloud protocol and cognitive walkthrough method—continue to influence HCI practice today. Lewis was elected to the CHI Academy in 2009, recognizing him for his contributions and impact in the field of HCI.

Clayton Lewis with Bonnie John at the INTERCHI Conference in Amsterdam, Netherlands in April 1993.

Lewis' current research interests include cognitive assistive technology, HCI, computers in education, and formal and computational models of mental processes. His recent work on technology designed for people with cognitive disabilities has been presented to the United States Access Board Technical Advisory Committee, the Rehabilitation Engineering and Assistive Technology Society of North America (RESNA), the International ACM SIGACCESS Conference on Computers and Accessibility (ACM ASSETS), and other forums.

Affiliations:

- ➤ Coleman-Turner Professor of Computer Science, University of Colorado (2018–2019)
- ➤ Fellow, Hanse-Wissenschaftskolleg, Delmenhorst, Germany (2017)
- ➤ Consultant, National Institute on Disability and Rehabilitation Research (2011–2014)
- ➤ Visiting Scientist, Knowledge Media Institute, The Open University, Milton Keynes, England (2008)
- ➤ Scientist in Residence, Coleman Institute for Cognitive Disabilities (2004–2011)
- ➤ Faculty Partner, IBM Printing Systems Division (2002)
- ➤ Chair, Department of Computer Science, University of Colorado (1999–2003)
- ➤ Professor, University of Colorado, Department of Computer Science (1992–Present)

Links:

- ➤ Homepage

J. C. R. LICKLIDER
FATHER OF THE INTERNET

J.C.R. Licklider, known as "Lick," was a computer visionary who had great influence on research directions though his leadership at ARPA and then MIT's Project MAC. He was soft spoken, but clear in promoting a human-centered approach to interactive systems design.

– Ben Shneiderman

J.C.R. Licklider is often referred to as "the father of the Internet" and "the Johnny Appleseed of computing." A pioneer in the advancement of computer science, Licklider had revolutionary vision for the relationship between humans and computers. At a time when most computers were large, cumbersome machines, Licklider saw the potential for computers to become desktop tools that would empower individuals, promote creativity, and facilitate communication and information sharing around the world.

Licklider speaking at the University of Maryland, College Park in April 1979.

Throughout his career, he advocated a human-centered approach to interactive systems design. His groundbreaking 1960 essay on "Man-Computer Symbiosis" emphasized how users "will set the goals, formulate the hypotheses, determine the criteria, and perform evaluations. Computing machines will do the routinizable work that must be done to prepare the way for insights and decisions in technical and scientific thinking."

Licklider also envisioned a computer network that would easily transfer and retrieve information. His idea led to the creation of ARPANET, which would evolve to become today's Internet.

Licklider talks with a colleague at the University of Maryland, College Park in April 1979.

Licklider's dream of "human-computer symbiosis" changed the course of computer science, paved the way into the modern landscape of computing, and ushered in the Internet age. However, given his humility and soft-spoken nature, Licklider never sought or achieved great recognition or widespread acclaim. He died in 1990 from complications following an asthma attack.

Affiliations:

➢ Professor Emeritus, MIT (1986–1990)

➢ Professor, MIT Laboratory for Computer Science (1975–1986)

➢ Director, MIT Project MAC and Professor of Electrical Engineering, MIT (1968–1970)

➢ Manager of Information Sciences, Systems, and Applications, Thomas J. Watson Center of International Business Machines (1964–1967)

➢ Director, Information Processing Techniques Office (IPTO) at the United States Department of Defense Advanced Research Projects Agency (DARPA) (1962)

➢ Vice President for psycho-acoustics, engineering psychology, and information systems, Bolt Beranek and Newman (1957–1962)

Links:

➢ Wikipedia

➢ Internet Hall of Fame Feature

➢ The Dream Machine: J.C.R. Licklider and the Revolution that Made Computing Personal, by M. Mitchell Waldrop

WENDY MACKAY
UBIQUITOUS COMPUTING PIONEER

Wendy Mackay has been a CHI Conference regular since 1983, consistently contributing to the organization of the conference. She served as General Chair in 2013 and brought a record number of attendees to the conference in her adopted hometown of Paris. Wendy also served SIGCHI in many other leadership positions, including becoming the Executive Chair. Her early work on the customizability of user interfaces revealed both the possibilities and the limitations. Later, she produced research on air traffic control systems, multimedia, family-oriented technology, email, and augmented reality. Wendy and her husband, Michel Beaudouin-Lafon, make a powerful team.

– Ben Shneiderman

Wendy Mackay is a Research Director (tenured Professor) at INRIA. She heads the ExSitu research group in HCI, which includes faculty, students, and research staff from INRIA, CNRS, and the University of Paris-Sud. She was formerly the Vice President of Research in Computer Science at the Université Paris-Sud. Her research focuses on the design of innovative interactive systems that truly meet the needs of their users.

Austin Henderson, Wendy Mackay, John Thomas, and Wendy Kellogg at the ACM CHI Conference on Human Factors in Computing Systems in Seattle, WA in 1990.

After studying experimental psychology, Mackay joined Digital Equipments Corporation (DEC), where she created a multimedia research group that produced the world's first commercial interactive video system (IVIS), a pre-Hypercard multimedia authoring language, and more than 30 multimedia projects. She has subsequently managed research groups at MIT, where she studied electronic mail and cognitive overload. She then joined Xerox PARC's EuroPARC, where she launched the area of ubiquitous computing. Along with her colleagues, she introduced the concept of augmented paper interfaces and explored how to integrate paper with online multimedia information.

Wendy Mackay at the ACM CHI Conference on Human Factors in Computing Systems in Paris, France, April 27–May 2, 2013.

Mackay's research interests include multidisciplinary and participatory design, mixed reality and interactive paper, situated interaction and co-adaptive systems, human-computer partnerships, and multimedia and mediated communication. She was elected to the CHI Academy in 2009, received the SIGCHI Lifetime Achievement Award in 2014, and was awarded a Doctor Honoris Causa from the University of Aarhus in 2017.

Affiliations:

> ➤ Research Director, Head of ExSitu, INRIA, Saclay, Île-de-France (2002–Present)

> ➤ Vice President, Computer Science Department, Université Paris-Sud, France (2007–2010)

> ➤ Senior Researcher, INRIA, Rocquencourt (2000–2002)

> ➤ Visiting Professor, Univ. Aarhus, Denmark (1998–2000)

> ➤ Senior Researcher, CENA (1996–1997)

Links:

> ➤ Homepage

> ➤ Wikipedia

AARON MARCUS
GROUNDBREAKER IN COMPUTER-BASED GRAPHIC DESIGN

Aaron Marcus is one of my closest professional friends going back to the days when I learned a lot from his two-day graphic design tutorial, which was part of a week-long mid-1980s course I organized at the University of Maryland. Aaron's frameworks and thousands of slides with examples of fonts, color palettes, aspect ratios, grids, and much more opened my eyes and changed my mind. We've shared family stories, enjoyed dinners together, and talked at length, whenever and wherever we could. When I needed help with design ideas, Aaron was often the person I turned to—he still is.

– Ben Shneiderman

Aaron Marcus is internationally recognized as an authority on the design of human-computer interfaces and electronic publishing documents. In 1967, Marcus became the first graphic designer in the world to work full-time with computer graphics as a summer researcher at AT&T's Bell Laboratories in New Jersey. He focused on the user interface as a major factor in implementing the user experience with computer-based products and services. By 1969, Marcus had become a computer graphics researcher and groundbreaking user-interface designer. In 1971–1973, he was the first professional designer to design virtual realities at Princeton University, using an Evans and Sutherland LDS-1 computer graphics system.

Aaron Marcus talks with a colleague at the ACM CHI Conference on Human Factors in Computing Systems in Boston, MA on December 11, 1983.

For about a decade, Marcus taught courses on computer graphics, design/visual communication, systematic design, information visualization, typography, and more at Princeton University. Marcus was the first professional designer to program virtual reality art/design spaces during his time as a faculty member at Princeton. Aaron Marcus's design/art works are in the collections of the San Francisco Museum of Modern Art, the Victoria and Albert Museum/

London, the Letterform Archive/San Francisco, the Computer History Museum/Mountain View, the RIT Vignelli Center for Graphic Design/Rochester, and the Berkeley Art Museum.

Marcus founded Aaron Marcus and Associates (AM+A), a user-interface design and consulting company, in 1982. It was one of the first such independent, computer-based graphic design firms in the world. Since 1989, Marcus shifted his focus to mobile devices, the Web, cross-cultural communication, and promoting good user-interface and information visualization design. The Association for Computing Machinery (ACM) Special Interest Group for Computer-Human Interaction (SIGCHI) elected Aaron Marcus to the CHI Academy, its highest honor, in 2009. Marcus was the first professional designer elected to this group.

Marcus at the HCI International Conference in Crete, Greece in June 2003.

Affiliations:

➢ Chair, DUXU15 (2015)

➢ Visiting Professor, College of Design and Innovation, Tongji University, Shanghai (2015)

➢ Master, De Tao Academy, Shanghai (2012)

➢ AIGA Fellow (2008)

➢ Founder and President, Aaron Marcus and Associates (AM+A) (1982–Present)

Links:

➢ ICOGRADA Graphic Design Hall of Fame

➢ Wikipedia

➢ IXDF Video Interview

➢ UX Pioneers Interview

S. JOY MOUNTFORD
USER EXPERIENCE AND INTERACTION DESIGN SPECIALIST

Joy Mountford's design and research leadership in Apple's Human Interface Group helped shape early ideas for many new products. I was a consultant for Apple in the late 1980s and enjoyed my visits to One Infinite Loop. Joy Mountford gave me a great opportunity during a 1993 visit, when I gave five talks in five days. It was great fun, and I learned a lot. Joy came to University of Maryland to speak in our User Interface Strategies 1990 satellite TV program. She gave the first ever live broadcast from a Mac which was exciting.

– Ben Shneiderman

S. Joy Mountford is an internationally recognized leader in the field of HCI who has designed and led teams responsible for developing a wide variety of systems. Mountford began her career as a designer at Honeywell, where she designed displays and controls for military aircraft, helmet display systems, and the space shuttle. While pursuing her graduate degree on a scholarship in aviation psychology, Mountford had learned how to use various flight simulators with extremely complex control systems. Her work at Honeywell improved the usability of such systems for many users.

Joy Mountford at the HCI International Conference in Boston, MA in 1989.

In the late 1980s, Mountford created and managed the acclaimed Human Interface Group at Apple Computer, the team that invented the initial use of QuickTime. She joined Interval Research in 1994 and served as a senior project lead on a series of musical and book development projects. Mountford went on to lead her own interaction design consulting company, building interactive products and website designs using data visualizations for a range of clients.

Mountford continues to serve as a consultant to a variety of companies and frequently teaches and presents at top conferences in the field, including ACM SIGCHI, IDCA, and TED.

She also promotes and challenges the next generation of interdisciplinary graduates through the International Design Expo. With various industry partners, it has sponsored design classes around the world for more than 20 years, creating a legacy of over 4000 students, now in influential industry and educational positions. While at Apple the Expo sponsored the classes that initiated the D school at Stanford and CRD at RCA.

Mountford with Brad Myers at the ACM CHI Conference on Human Factors in Computing Systems in Austin, TX in May 2012.

SIGCHI awarded Mountford the 2012 Lifetime Practice Award for her outstanding contributions to the practice and understanding of HCI.

Affiliations:

➢ Senior Director, Akamai Technologies (2012–2015)

➢ Osher Fellow, Exploratorium (2011–2011)

➢ Founder and Director, Interaction Design Expo (1989–2011)

➢ Vice President of User Experience Design, Yahoo! (2005–2008)

➢ Founder and Principal, idbias (2000–2005)

Links:

➢ Wikipedia

➢ LinkedIn

BRAD MYERS
USER INTERFACE SOFTWARE ENGINEER

I'm constantly in admiration of Brad's terrifically prolific contributions to the software engineering aspects of user interface design. His series of jewel-named projects (Amethyst, Peridot, Garnet, etc.) helped push forward many user interface innovations and developer tools. Brad's encyclopedic knowledge of the field were put to good use in his masterful 2-hour video called "All the Widgets," which captured many early designs for everyone to see and learn from. His broad knowledge (and strong writing skills) are visible in his 1996 review "A Brief History of Human-Computer Interaction Technology." Brad has been an influential teacher, producing a stream of doctoral students who have gone on to do important work on their own. One memorable event was when we (and two others) went to ACM headquarters to successfully argue for the creation of the ACM Interactions magazine. Let me close by saying how generous Brad has been in organizing conferences, editing journals, running awards programs, and helping students. I give a lot of credit to Brad for helping make HCI so successful—his impact has been enormous in technically rigorous research plus his strong service and effective education.

– Ben Shneiderman

Brad Myers is a Professor in the Human-Computer Interaction Institute in the School of Computer Science at Carnegie Mellon University.

He is the author or editor of over 500 publications, including the books *Creating User Interfaces by Demonstration* and *Languages for Developing User Interfaces*, and he has been on the editorial board of six journals. He has been a consultant on user interface design and implementation to over 85 companies, and regularly teaches courses on user interface design and software. His research interests include user interfaces, programming environments, programming language design, end-user software engineering (EUSE), API usability, developer experience (DevX or DX), interaction techniques, programming by example, handheld computers, and visual programming.

Myers with Bill Buxton, Terry Winograd, and Ron Baecker (left to right) at the CHI 2005 event in Portland, Oregon in April 2005.

He received the ACM SIGCHI Lifetime Research Award in Research in 2017, for "outstanding fundamental and influential research contributions to the study of human-computer interaction." He is an IEEE Fellow, ACM Fellow, member of the CHI Academy, and winner of 13 Best Paper type awards and 5 Most Influential Paper Awards.

Affiliations:

➢ Faculty Member, School of Computer Science at Carnegie Mellon University (1987–Present); Professor, Human-Computer Interaction Institute, School of Computer Science (2004–Present)

➢ Advisor UI/UX, PIXterity (2012–Present)

➢ Strategic User Interface Advisor, Web and Mobile, SachManya LLC (2010–Present)

➢ Consultant, more than 85 companies including Desmarais LLP, Silicon Valley Expert Witness Group Inc., Apple Computer, Inc. and the Institute for Defense Analyses (1984–Present)

Links:

➢ Homepage

➢ Wikipedia

ELIZABETH MYNATT
EVERYDAY COMPUTING EXPERT

Elizabeth Mynatt was trained in a supportive community—including her advisor, Jim Foley, in particular—that already valued human-centered computing. She has maintained her connection with Georgia Tech as she went from junior to senior roles, taking on leadership for the Institute for People and Technology and on a national level within the Computing Research Association. Through focused efforts and hard work, she now inspires the next generation of HCI researchers with sensitivity to family, home, and community.

– Ben Shneiderman

Elizabeth "Beth" Mynatt is the executive director of the Institute for People and Technology (IPaT) and a professor in the College of Computing at the Georgia Institute of Technology. IPaT serves as a catalyst connecting industry, government, and non-profit leaders with Georgia Tech researchers to advance transformations in media, health, education, enterprises, and humanitarian systems. Mynatt also founded and directs Georgia Tech's Everyday Computing Lab, which examines the human-computer interface implications of computation permeating many aspects of everyday life. Mynatt is internationally recognized for her expertise in areas of ubiquitous computing, personal health informatics, computer-supported collaborative work, and human-computer interface design.

Elizabeth Mynatt with Jennifer Preece and Elizabeth Churchill at the ACM CHI Conference on Human Factors in Computing Systems in Toronto, Canada, April 26–May 1, 2014.

From 2005–2010, Mynatt directed the GVU Center, one of the most prominent interdisciplinary research centers focusing on HCI, ubiquitous computing, graphics, wearable computing, and computer-supported cooperative work, among other areas. She has continued her work with the GVU Center as a professor and one of the principal researchers on the Aware Home Research Initiative, investigating the development of future home technologies.

The Initiative particularly focuses on technologies that would enable older adults to continue living independently, rather than seeking care in an institutional setting. Mynatt has made notable contributions to the development of cognitive prosthesis and technology support for chronic health care.

Elizabeth Mynatt with Duncan Watts (left) and Scott Hudson (right) at the Computer Sciences and Telecommunications Board Workshop on Continuing Innovation in Information Technology on March 5, 2015 in Washington, DC.

Mynatt was elected to the CHI Academy in 2009 and chaired the 2010 ACM CHI Conference on Human Factors in Computing Systems. In 2015, Mynatt was named an ACM Fellow "for contributions to human-centered computing and to the development of health information technologies."

Affiliations:

➤ Vice Chair, Computing Community Consortium (2014–Present)

➤ Member, Microsoft Research's Technical Advisory Board (2012–2014)

➤ Executive Director of the Institute for People and Technology (2011–Present) and Professor (1998–Present), Georgia Tech

➤ Director, GVU Center, Georgia Tech (2005–2010)

Links:

➤ Homepage

➤ Wikipedia

TED NELSON
VISIONARY OF UNIVERSAL HYPERTEXT SYSTEMS

A pioneering visionary of universal hypertext systems including the social and legal structures; keynote speaker at Hypertext '87 Workshop. Ted Nelson's creative visions are amply displayed in his lively books, Computer Lib/Dream Machines *and* Literary Machines, *which detail his hypertext vision. Nelson understood that major social and legal changes would be necessary to realize his concept of universal hypertext environment. His XANADU system supported enormous "docuverses" including complex links among literary sources, quotations, critiques, etc. and a vast global network accessible from community-oriented computer centers.*

– Ben Shneiderman

Theodor "Ted" Nelson is a sociologist, philosopher, and pioneer of information technology. He founded his most prominent project, Xanadu, in 1960 with the goal of escaping the prison of paper and creating new forms of unprintable documents with visible connections between pages. Project Xanadu was intended to be a worldwide electronic publishing system that would have created in essence a universal library for the public, "a magic place of literary memory." Nelson documented his work on the project in his books *Computer Lib/Dream Machines* (1974) and *Literary Machines* (1981).

Despite Nelson's efforts and unwavering vision, Project Xanadu has not materialized. Nonetheless, Project Xanadu's intellectual presence in the field influenced research and catalyzed the evolution of hypertext systems.

Nelson with Jennifer Preece (center) and Marlene Mallicoat (right) at the Oxford Internet Institute in June 2006.

Nelson is also credited with coining the terms "hypertext" and "hypermedia" in 1963 and publishing the terms in 1965. The first uses of the words transclusion, virtuality, intertwingularity, and dildonics are also attributed to Nelson.

Nelson with Ben Shneiderman, pointing out that Nelson is No. 1, at the Oxford Internet Institute in June 2006.

Nelson's creative impact has been recognized in the 1998 Yuri Rubinsky Memorial Web Award, World Wide Web Conference, which is "… presented to an individual who has a lifetime of achievement in the 'care and feeding' of the global information infrastructure." He was knighted by France in 2001 as "Officier des Arts et Lettres," which is "…presented to individuals achieving distinction in the arts and literature throughout the world."

In 2014, SIGCHI awarded Nelson a Special Recognition Award, which recognizes individuals whose vision or achievements have significantly influenced and broadly shaped conceptions of HCI. The ACM Special Interest Group on Hypertext and the Web presents the Ted Nelson Newcomer Award at its annual conference for the best paper written by authors who have never published in earlier Hypertext proceedings.

Affiliations:

> ➤ Visiting Professor, University of Southampton, England (2012)

> ➤ Visiting Fellow, Oxford Internet Institute (2004–2006)

> ➤ Visiting Fellow, Wadham College, Oxford (2004–2006)

> ➤ Co-Founder, Itty bitty machine company (ibm) (1977–1980)

> ➤ Founder, Project Xanadu (1960–Present)

Links:

> ➤ Homepage

> ➤ Wikipedia

ALAN NEWELL
ADVOCATE FOR THE "DIGITALLY DISADVANTAGED"

Alan's long history of research and design for older adults and users with disabilities inspired me and many others. In writing the foreword for his book that summarized his career, I learned even more about his varied contributions and appreciated the value of his work. His smiling cheerful spirit is infectious.

– Ben Shneiderman

Alan Newell, an Emeritus Professor at Dundee University, has conducted research in the field of HCI for more than 40 years, primarily focusing on supporting the elderly and people with disabilities. He founded the University's School of Computing and established its Queen Mother Research Centre, one of the largest academic groups in the world dedicated to researching systems for the elderly and disabled people.

Newell with Beth Mynatt and Peter Gregor at the Assistive Technologies – ACM Special Interest Group on Computers and the Physically Handicapped event in Arlington, VA in November 2000.

Together with colleagues, Newell developed stenograph transcription systems, television subtitling systems for deaf and hearing-impaired people, and a wide range of communications systems for non-speaking people. As technology became increasingly pervasive in everyday life, Newell took notice of the people—particularly older people—who found those new technologies frightening, confusing, and difficult to use.

Newell asserted that designers must be aware of the needs and characteristics of all user groups, including "digitally disadvantaged people," in order to develop successful technologies. In collaboration with theatre professionals, Newell and other HCI researchers produced a range of films and interactive live theatre productions as part of requirements gathering exercises, to raise awareness of the challenges that "digitally disadvantaged people" face and to encourage students and designers to develop empathy for them.

Loren Terveen presents the SIGCHI Social Impact Award to Alan Newell at the ACM Conference on Human Factors in Computing Systems in Vancouver, BC Canada in May 2011.

Newell is widely published and has delivered numerous keynote lectures at conferences in North America, Europe, and Japan. He was named an ACM Fellow in 2006 for his "contribution to computer-based systems for people with disabilities" and was awarded the CHI Social Impact Award in 2011. The CHI Academy inducted Newell in 2012.

Affiliations:

> ➤ Emeritus Professor, Dundee University, Scotland

> ➤ Deputy Principal, Dundee University

> ➤ Member, Order of the British Empire

Links:

> ➤ Homepage

ALLEN NEWELL
PIONEER OF ARTIFICIAL INTELLIGENCE

One of the great thinkers about people and machines. He was a hero with whom I planned to do my graduate studies in 1968, but the Vietnam War interfered with that. My draft board would not approve a deferment for me to accept a fellowship to study with Newell, so I spent three years teaching data processing at SUNY-Farmingdale (a two-year community college), which is how I came to do my graduate work at SUNY-Stony Brook. I followed Newell's work closely, and occasionally met him at conferences. One of my great moments was when in 1985 in his CHI Conference keynote, Newell favorably mentioned my 1980 book on Software Psychology. His deep thinking about human psychology were a strong inspiration during my development.

– Ben Shneiderman

Allen Newell was a computer scientist and renowned pioneer of AI. In 1975, Newell and his long-time collaborator, Herbert A. Simon, won the A.M. Turing Award, the highest honor in computer science, for their "contributions to AI, the psychology of human cognition, and list processing."

Alan Newell sits with Sylvia Shepard, Bill Curtis, and Stu Card (left to right) at the ACM CHI Conference on Human Factors in Computing Systems in San Francisco, CA on April 14, 1985.

Newell's ultimate goal was to understand how humans think and to build systems that would enable humans to solve concrete, real-world problems. While working with the RAND Corporation in 1952,

Newell began discussing how computers could be used to examine human problem-solving techniques with Simon, a RAND consultant on organizational analysis. In 1956, Newell and Simon, in collaboration with RAND colleague Clifford Shaw, produced one of the first artificial programs, Logic Theorist.

Newell and Simon also invented the Information Processing Language (IPL) for the Logic Theorist and other AI programs. The partners unveiled their next project, the General Problem Solver (GPS), in 1957. This program would apply modifiable "rules of thumb" to a given problem, then perform a "means-ends" analysis after each step to determine if it was closer to achieving the desired solution.

After leaving RAND in 1961, Newell joined the faculty at Carnegie Institute of Technology (now Carnegie Mellon University) and contributed to the creation of one of the first computer science departments in the United States. Newell continued to dedicate his research to understanding human cognition and building systems to solve problems. He became the founding president of the American Association for Artificial Intelligence (1979–1980) and was awarded the U.S. National Medal of Science just before he died of cancer in 1992.

Newell talks with Don Norman (left) at the ACM CHI Conference on Human Factors in Computing Systems in San Francisco, CA on April 14, 1985.

Affiliations:

➢ Professor of Computer Science and Psychology, Carnegie Mellon (1961–1992)

➢ RAND Corporation (1950–1961)

Links:

➢ Wikipedia

➢ Encyclopaedia Britannica

JACOB NIELSEN
WEB PAGE USABILITY GURU

I remember meeting Jakob as a young Scandinavian researcher who I invited to attend my week-long course in 1985 (or 1986?). He went on to become the most famous promoter of HCI thinking through his professional talks around the world, his widely read AlertBox articles are often bold, playful, and clever. I am always ready to defend Jakob against his critics, and think we need ten more Jakob's to help promote HCI. He came to speak for my User Interface Strategies '94 satellite TV show (December 1993) and I was happy to join him, Don Norman, and Brenda Laurel for a speaking tour to London and Amsterdam (April 2000).

– Ben Shneiderman

Jakob Nielsen is a user advocate and principal of the Nielsen Norman Group, a user experience consulting firm he co-founded with Dr. Donald A. Norman in 1998. *The New York Times* has called Nielsen "the guru of Web page usability," and he was named "the world's leading expert on Web usability" by *U.S. News and World Report*. Nielsen holds 79 U.S. patents, mainly on ways to make the Internet easier to use.

Nielsen at the HCI International Conference in Honolulu, HI in August 1987.

While working as an assistant professor at the Technical University of Denmark, Nielsen established the "discount usability engineering" movement, offering HCI researchers a simpler, cheaper way to evaluate and improve usability. The idea was born out of necessity—his budget as an academic was much smaller than the funds available to industry researchers. He advocated three pillars of discount usability: simplified user testing with five participants, narrowed-down paper prototypes, and heuristic evaluation, in which researchers evaluate user interface designs by assessing them relative to established usability guidelines.

Nielsen presents at the ACM CHI Conference on Human Factors in Computing Systems in Denver, CO in May 1995.

Nielsen is the author of many widely renowned titles, including the best-selling book *Designing Web Usability: The Practice of Simplicity*, which has sold more than a quarter of a million copies in 22 languages. He was inducted into the Scandinavian Interactive Media Hall of Fame in 2000 and elected to the ACM CHI Academy in 2006.

Nielsen also received the SIGCHI Lifetime Achievement Award for Human-Computer Interaction Practice in 2013.

Affiliations:

➤ Principal, Nielsen Norman Group (1998–Present)

➤ Distinguished Engineer, Sun Microsystems (1994–1998)

➤ Member of Research Staff, Bellcore (1990–1994)

Links:

➤ Homepage

➤ Wikipedia

DON NORMAN
MENTOR AND PIONEER

Don is a senior colleague whose early work on cognitive psychology and book on User Centered System Design *were influential to me and many others. He became a fierce critic of problems in user interface designs, raising concerns at conferences and writing thoughtful books that often wisely guided designers to think deeper. He was a helpful mentor, who I appreciated talking with at conferences. I also enjoyed photographing Don because of his expressive body language and engaging speaking style.*

– Ben Shneiderman

Don Norman is both a businessman—a former Vice President at Apple and Executive at Hewlett-Packard—and an academic, having served as a faculty member at Harvard, University of California at San Diego, Northwestern, and KAIST in South Korea. He is best known for his work in usability engineering, cognitive science, and design strategy. His most recent work emphasizes how designers can contribute to driving gradual and radical innovation within companies.

Norman talks with Clayton Lewis (left) and John Seeley Brown (right) at the ACM CHI Conference on Human Factors in Computing Systems in December 1983 in Boston, MA.

Norman recently established the Design Lab at the University of California, San Diego, which promotes a novel convergence of practice and theory, of Thinking, Observing, and Making: TOM. The Design Lab aims to let TOM define its approach to producing products, services, and systems that advance the state of knowledge and benefit the public. Norman serves as Director of the Design Lab and professor emeritus of psychology, cognitive science, and electrical and computer engineering.

Norman speaks at the Nielsen's Lecture Tour event in London, England on March 3, 2000.

He is also co-founder and principal of the user experience/usability consulting firm the Nielsen Norman group, through which Norman coordinates his work as a consultant and keynote speaker. Companies frequently seek out Norman's expertise in making products more enjoyable, understandable, and profitable.

Norman received the CHI Lifetime Achievement Award, SIGCHI's most prestigious honor, in 2002. In 2011, he was elected to the National Academy of Engineering, recognizing him "for development of design principles based on human cognition that enhance the interaction between people and technology."

His books include *Emotional Design*, *Living with Complexity*, and the hugely successful *The Design of Everyday Things: Revised and Expanded*.

Affiliations:

- ➤ Board of Trustees, IIT's Institute of Design in Chicago (2014–Present)
- ➤ Founder and Director, The Design Lab at University of California, San Diego (Present)
- ➤ Co-founder and Principal, Nielsen Norman Group (1998–Present)
- ➤ IDEO Fellow, IDEO (2011–Present)
- ➤ Professor of Computer Science, Northwestern University (2001–2010), Co-Founder Segal Design Institute, Co-Director MBA program, Breed Professor of Design

Links:

- ➤ Homepage
- ➤ Wikipedia

DAN OLSEN
USER INTERFACE SOFTWARE PIONEER

*Dan Olsen has been intensely devoted to the SIGCHI commu-
nity, bringing his cheerful laugh and strong opinions, while
working hard for all his career to raise quality and support
students. He's an admirable community builder and his own
work on software engineering tools to support developers had
widespread impact on the tools now so widely used.*

– Ben Shneiderman

Dan Olsen Jr., formerly a Professor of Computer Science at Brigham Young University, is one of
the first and most influential researchers specializing in user interface software. His research contri-
butions span a wide variety of areas, including Computer Supported Cooperative Work, Interactive
Machine Learning, and the development of metrics and principles for human-robot interaction.
Olsen also served as the first director of the Human-Computer Interaction Institute at Carnegie
Mellon University.

*Dan Olsen with John Sibert and Brad Myers
(left to right) at the ACM CHI Conference
on Human Factors in Computing Systems in
Boston, MA on April 24, 1994.*

At Brigham Young University, Olsen directed the Interactive Computing Everywhere
(ICE) Project, which aims to provide people with
interactive access to computer technology in every physical situation involving work or play. As
the cost of computing decreases, while the power and capabilities of such technologies increase,
computing has potential to permeate more of people's everyday lives. As people began to use new
computing and interactive devices in new situations, the resulting diversity of interactive capabili-

ties—and the management of this diversity—posed a key challenge for researchers such as Olsen and his ICE project team.

Olsen's additional research interests include QuizTek, a project to automate grading through interactive machine learning; Physical Computing, developing new devices with embedded computation; and Wyldlight, an effort to capture light, shape, and motion in the natural world.

Dan Olsen with Marilyn Tremaine at the ACM CHI Conference on Human Factors in Computing Systems in The Hague, The Netherlands in April 2000.

In 2002, Olsen received the CHI Lifetime Service Award, recognizing his many years of work on behalf of the SIGCHI community and his initiatives to benefit his colleagues, including playing a key role in founding the highly successful Annual ACM Symposium on User Interface Software and Technology (UIST). He was inducted into the CHI Academy in 2004 and awarded the CHI Lifetime Research Award in 2012.

Affiliations:

- ➤ Professor, Brigham Young University (1990–Present)
- ➤ Director, Human-Computer Interaction Institute, Carnegie Mellon University (1996–1998)
- ➤ Professor, Carnegie Mellon University (1996–1998)

Links:

- ➤ Wikipedia

GARY OLSON
COLLABORATION EXPERT

Gary's playful side complemented his serious research side, making him an appealing colleague. He and Judy wrote the influential paper on "Distance Matters" (2000) about how even in the age of internet communications, it was easier to collaborate face-to-face than remotely. Gary focused on Scientific Collaboration on the Internet (his co-edited 2008 book), studying and helping collaboratories succeed. He admirably put in a lot of energy into community building efforts, especially the SIGCHI Executive Committee—he's a real team player.

– Ben Shneiderman

Gary Olson is a Donald Bren Professor of Information and Computer Sciences at the University of California, Irvine and Professor Emeritus at the University of Michigan. He is a cognitive psychologist whose research primarily focuses on how people collaborate to complete complex intellectual projects. Using both laboratory and field studies to explore the fields of programming, design, and science, Olson has produced perhaps the most extensive program of research on collaboration over distance.

Gary and Judy Olson at the ACM CHI Conference on Human Factors in Computing Systems in Toronto, Canada in April 1987.

Olson has led the nation in the development and study of "collaboratories"—a concept formed in the late 1980s and defined as a "center without walls" in which researchers who were geographically dispersed could work together using appropriate technologies to access one another, databases, and other shared tools. Olson not only studied collaboration, but also practiced it with his long-time collaborator and wife, Judith "Judy" Olson. The couple produced a long series of papers describing the technology design principles and social conditions conducive to effective collaboration over distance, including their classic paper "Distance Matters."

Olson with Wendy Kellogg (left) and Jennifer Preece (right) at the ACM CHI Conference on Human Factors in Computing Systems in Minneapolis, MN in April 2002.

Gary Olson was elected to the CHI Academy in 2003, recognizing him for his independent contributions to the field, including editing a range of top journals and chairing some of SIGCHI's most prominent conferences. In 2006, SIGCHI presented its most prestigious award, The Lifetime Achievement Award, to the joint team of Gary and Judy Olson to honor "their long, productive collaboration as a single, unique contribution to the field of computer-human Interaction, or perhaps more accurately, of human-human collaboration, mediated and enhanced through modern technologies." Gary Olson also received ACM SIGCHI's Lifetime Service Award in 2016.

Affiliations:

> Donald Bren Professor of Information and Computer Sciences, University of California, Irvine (2008–2016)

> Emeritus Professor, University of Michigan (2008–Present)

> Visiting Researcher, Microsoft Research (2003)

> Paul M. Fitts Professor of Human-Computer Interaction, School of Information, University of Michigan (2000–2008)

Links:

> Homepage

JUDY OLSON
COLLABORATION OVER DISTANCE PIONEER

Judy made the transition from psychology to HCI in the early 1980s and became the consistent promoter of computer supported collaborative work. Judy came to speak for my User Interface Strategies '94 satellite TV show (December 1993) and left a strong impression on me. She and Gary wrote the influential paper on "Distance Matters" (2000) about how even in the age of internet communications, it was easier to collaborate face-to-face than remotely. Judy's strong business understanding made her an effective leader and advocate for HCI.

– Ben Shneiderman

Judith "Judy" Olson is a Donald Bren Professor of Information and Computer Sciences in the School of Information and Computer Sciences, the School of Social Ecology, and the Merage School of Business at the University of California, Irvine. Her areas of expertise include technology in the workplace, information science, and psychology. She is renowned in the field of HCI for her pioneering research on how geographically dispersed teams work together and how communication technology can better support their work.

Judy Olson at the ACM CHI Conference on Human Factors in Computing Systems in Boston, MA in April 1986.

The recurring theme throughout her career has been her focus on technology for long-distance collaboration, including video conferencing, ShrEdit (an equivalent of Google Docs), and other groupware tools. Olson conducted research that combined fieldwork, lab experiments, and agent-based simulations to determine how to help new scientific collaborations succeed. Her laboratory studies specifically focused on the communication challenges facing teams working over distances and the resulting underutilization of remote team members and loss of trust. Olson was elected to the inaugural class of the CHI Academy in 2001 and was awarded the Athena Lecture from ACM-W, the equivalent of a "Woman of the Year" in computer science, in 2011–2012.

Gary and Judy Olson at the ACM CHI Conference on Human Factors in Computing Systems in May 2011 in Vancouver, BC Canada.

Olson is not only an expert on collaboration, but also an expert collaborator. She and her husband, Gary Olson, produced a series of papers articulating the technology design principles and social conditions that foster effective collaboration over distance, including their widely cited paper, "Distance Matters." In 2006, SIGCHI presented its most prestigious award, The Lifetime Achievement Award, to the joint team of Gary and Judy Olson to honor "their long, productive collaboration as a single, unique contribution to the field of computer-human interaction, or perhaps more accurately, of human-human collaboration, mediated and enhanced through modern technologies." In 2018, she was elected to the National Academy of Engineering.

Affiliations:

> Donald Bren Professor of Information and Computer Science, Professor in the Paul Merage School of Business, and Professor in the School of Social Ecology, University of California, Irvine (2008–Present)

> Professor Emerita, University of Michigan (2008–Present)

> Associate Dean for Academic Affairs, School of Information, University of Michigan (2006–2008)

Links:

> Homepage

> Wikipedia

RANDY PAUSCH
VIRTUAL REALITY PIONEER

Randy Pausch's energetic style and prolific publication record made him a quickly rising young star. He made noticeable advances with his user interface software engineering tools, virtual reality systems (Worlds in Miniature and Virtual Reality on $5 a Day), and an innovative 3D animation system (Alice) for teaching programming. His work with Disney Imagineering brought fresh ideas to the user interface and the entertainment communities. Randy's enthusiasm and passion was infectious, attracting students and devoted fans, including me. He often made clever, powerful comments about research and life, such as this memorable quote: "When people are arguing about apples or oranges, bring them a watermelon." He courageously fought pancreatic cancer and shared his story through the inspirational and moving Last Lecture: Really Achieving Your Childhood Dreams (September 18, 2007), which has been viewed more than 18 million times. Randy holds a special place in my professional memories—he still makes me smile and pushes me to do better.

– Ben Shneiderman

Randy Pausch was a Professor of Computer Science, Human-Computer Interaction, and Design at Carnegie Mellon, where he was the co-founder of Carnegie Mellon's Entertainment Technology Center (ETC). He brought together artists, dramatists, designers, and computer scientists to create innovative technology. He was a National Science Foundation Presidential Young Investigator and a Lilly Foundation Teaching Fellow.

Pausch was the driving force behind the virtual world programming environment "Alice" and its "playful learning" pedagogy. It enables college, high school, and middle school students to develop their own characters in 3D virtual worlds and modify the behavior of those characters. He extended the project with "Storytelling Alice," which gave middle school girls a positive first experience with computer programming. He wrote a book on the project, which is currently in use at more than 250 colleges and universities. He also created the Simple User Interface Toolkit (SUIT) for formal user testing of theme park attractions and co-founded the Carnegie Mellon Entertainment Technology Center at CMU, which offers the world's only Master of Entertainment Technology degree.

Randy Pausch talking with Marc Brown at the ACM CHI Conference on Human Factors in Computing Systems in Seattle, WA in 1990.

He did sabbaticals at Walt Disney Imagineering and Electronic Arts (EA) and consulted with Google on user interface design. Pausch received his bachelor's degree in Computer Science from Brown University and his Ph.D. in Computer Science from Carnegie Mellon University. He authored or co-authored 5 books and more than 70 articles. He was a pioneer in the development of virtual reality, having designed the "Building Virtual Worlds" class at CMU.

He is famous outside of academia due to his inspiring speech in "The Last Lecture," where he spoke on how he achieved his childhood dreams and shared insights on how to live a good life. He died of pancreatic cancer on July 24, 2008.

Affiliations:

- Professor (2000–2008), Co-Director of the Entertainment Technology Center (1998–2008), Associate Professor (1997–2000), Carnegie Mellon University

- Sabbatical with Walt Disney Imagineering Virtual Reality Studio (1995)

- Associate Professor of Computer Science (1993–1997), Assistant Professor (1988–1993), University of Virginia

Links:

- Carnegie Mellon University's tribute to Pausch after his death

- Wikipedia

CATHERINE PLAISANT
USER INTERFACE EXPERT

Catherine has been my close collaborator since 1987, as we worked together to write 100+ papers, often with UMD Computer Science graduate students who we jointly supervised. As a Research Scientist, she complemented my professorial role in supervising students, connecting with companies, and conducting rigorous studies. We often had constructive differences of opinion, leading to respectful discussions that pushed our thinking forward. May you all be so fortunate as to have a creative research collaborator (and a friend) as wonderful as Catherine.

– Ben Shneiderman

Catherine Plaisant is a Senior Research Scientist at the University of Maryland Institute for Advanced Computer Studies and the Associate Director of Research of the Human-Computer Interaction Lab. She earned a Doctorat d'Ingenieur in 1982 and traveled to the United States in 1988 to join Professor of Computer Science Ben Shneiderman at the Human-Computer Interaction Lab (HCIL), where she continues to work with multidisciplinary teams to design and evaluate new technologies and user interfaces.

Plaisant with Stephane Chatty and Christophe Tronche at the INTERCHI Conference in Amsterdam, Netherlands in April 1993.

Before joining HCIL, Plaisant worked in Paris, France at the Centre Mondial Informatique et Ressources Humaines. She developed learning environments for pre-school children and conducted evaluations in classrooms. During her time with HCIL, her research contributions have included: focused user interaction techniques, such as Excentric Labeling; innovative visualizations, such as LifeLines for personal records or SpaceTree for hierarchical data exploration; and interactive search interface techniques, including Query Previews.

Plaisant's recent research projects include novel designs for electronic health record systems and visual analytics environments for the analysis of temporal event sequences. Plaisant has written more than 200 published papers on subjects ranging from information visualization to medical informatics to technology for families. She became co-author for the 4th, 5th, and 6th editions of *Designing the User Interface*, among the most prominent books on HCI. Plaisant was elected to the CHI Academy in 2015.

Catherine Plaisant with long-time collaborator Ben Shneiderman at the HCIL Annual Symposium at the University of Maryland in College Park on May 26, 2011.

Affiliations:

➢ INRIA International Chair (2018–2022)

➢ Affiliate Senior Research Scientist, College of Information Studies, University of Maryland's iSchool (2012–Present)

➢ Associate Member, Center for the Advanced Study of Language (2009–Present)

➢ Associate Director of Research, Human-Computer Interaction Laboratory (1997–Present)

Links:

➢ Homepage

➢ Wikipedia

JENNIFER PREECE
ONLINE SOCIAL INTERACTION RESEARCHER

I first met Jenny in 1992, when she sought to interview me at a conference in Halifax, Nova Scotia for her influential HCI book. Then, when I saw her again at the CHI 1993 Conference in Amsterdam and told her about my sad divorce story, she replied that she was in the same situation. That led to longer discussions and a deepening relationship. She moved to the U.S. in December 1996, and we were happily married in 2001. She's continued writing her HCI books, plus her pioneering book on Online Communities, so we have common ground for discussions, but we mostly work to help each other, rather than to collaborate. She was Dean of the iSchool at the University of Maryland (2005-2015, the Provost called her an "Outstanding Dean") and her current research is breaking new ground in HCI for citizen science. It's been a wonderful time together.

– Ben Shneiderman

Jennifer "Jenny" Preece is a professor and former Dean of the College of Information Studies at the University of Maryland, College Park. She researches online communities, specifically identifying what makes such communities successful and how usability factors impact social behaviors online.

Preece with Charles Lowry (left) and William Destler (right) at the celebration welcoming her as the Dean of the College of Information Studies at the University of Maryland, College Park in September 2005.

In the early 1990s, Preece began to focus on the design and management of digital social media. She became fascinated with determining the motives behind participation in social media and examining the relationship between usability and sociability. During her research, Preece observed a high level of empathy in some online communities—particularly patient support spaces—for which she coined the term "empathic communities."

This led to the publication of one of the first books on online communities in 2000, *Online Communities: Designing Usability, Supporting Sociability* published by John Wiley and Sons. Beginning in 2009, her focus shifted to the study of how technology could foster citizen science. Preece aims to understand and harness various motives for long-term citizen engagement and to support diversity in public participation in science.

Preece began a 30-year collaboration with Yvonne Rogers and Helen Sharp, when they worked together on the first distance education course in HCI at the British Open University. This led to their first successful book entitled *Human-Computer Interaction*, published in 1994. Preece continues to work with her co-authors on the successive editions of *Interaction Design: Beyond HCI*, which will be launched in its 5th edition in 2019.

Yvonne Rogers (left), Helen Sharp (center), and Preece at their book party at the ACM CHI Conference on Human Factors in Computing Systems in Vancouver, BC, Canada in 2011.

Affiliations:

➢ Professor, University of Maryland, College of Information Studies (2015–current)

➢ Professor and Dean, University of Maryland, College of Information Studies (2004–2015)

➢ Professor and Department Chair, University of Maryland Baltimore County, Information Systems Department (1997–2004)

Links:

➢ Wikipedia

GEORGE ROBERTSON
PIONEER OF INFORMATION VISUALIZATION

George Robertson's superb design and implementation skills for 3D environments helped create pioneering interactive experiences that were eye-catching and influential. I always respected his contributions, although I sometimes had lively discussions with George when I questioned if 3D was the right approach. His work remains highly referenced, and he remains a great colleague.

– Ben Shneiderman

George Robertson is one of the founders of Information Visualization, a field in which users perceive patterns in visual presentations of complex information. He developed several Information Visualization techniques that have become widely used in the field. Before retiring in 2011, Robertson had been a faculty member in Carnegie Mellon University's Computer Science Department and worked with Thinking Machines, Xerox PARC, Microsoft Research, and Bolt Beranek and Newman.

Robertson's work contributed to a wide variety of areas in computer science, including hospital information systems, operating systems, and programming languages. In collaboration with Allen Newell and Don McCracken, Robertson designed the L* programming language, which was interactive, rather than compiler-based. He also designed one of the earliest hypertext systems, called ZOG, in 1972. It was a rapid-response, large-network menu selection system that greatly improved man-machine communication. He was the principal investigator on an ARPA contract investigating system architectures for archival memory, including the design of two file systems. He designed the Accent operating system (predecessor to the GNU Mach) with Rick Rashid and built the first microkernel-based operating system.

Robertson holds 103 patents on information technology and 3 patents on the design of the second-generation Connection Machine. He was one of the designers of Diamond, the world's first multimedia message system, and did research on distributed systems. He developed a number of visualization and 3D user interface systems at Xerox PARC and Microsoft Research.

Catherine Plaisant, Ben Shneiderman, Robert Spence, George Robertson, Ernest Edmonds, and Linda Candy (left to right) at the ACM CHI Conference on Human Factors in Computing Systems in Seattle, WA, March 31–April 5, 2001.

Robertson did pioneering work on animated 3D user interfaces for intelligent information access and was the architect of the Information Visualizer. He invented novel 3D interaction techniques and a number of visualization techniques, including Cone Trees, the Perspective Wall, the Spiral Visualization, the Document Lens, the WebBook, and the Web Forager.

He served on the Advisory Board of the Department of Homeland Security National Visualization and Analytics Center from 2004–2011. He has also served on program committees for a number of conferences. He was Conference Chair of IEEE Information Visualization 2004 and Symposium Chair of ACM User Interface Software and Technology 1997. He served as associate editor for *ACM Transactions on Information Systems* from 2004–2009. He currently serves as associate editor for *Information Visualization*, an international journal published by Palgrave/Macmillan.

In 2002, he was elected an ACM Fellow. He was elected to the CHI Academy in 2006 and received the ACM SIGCHI Lifetime Research Achievement Award in 2013.

Affiliations:

- ➤ Principal Researcher (2006–2011), Partner (2000–2011), Senior Researcher (1996–2006), Manager of User Interface Research (1996–1999), Microsoft Research

- ➤ Principal Scientist, Xerox PARC (1988–1996)

- ➤ Senior Scientist, Thinking Machines Corporation (1984–1988)

Links:

- ➤ Wikipedia

- ➤ Infovis page

- ➤ L Star System

YVONNE ROGERS
UBIQUITOUS COMPUTING PIONEER

The best word for Yvonne is "sharp" in her thinking. She pushes me and others to think more deeply, shows fresh ways of looking at problems, and writes with compelling clarity about the latest directions and theories in HCI. Her participation with Helen Sharp and Jennifer Preece to write Interaction Design *helped make it one of the most widely used HCI text-books.*

– Ben Shneiderman

Yvonne Rogers is the director of The University College London Interaction Centre (UCLIC), the leading UK Centre of Excellence in HCI teaching and research. She also teaches courses as a Professor of Interaction Design and serves as a deputy head of the Computer Science Department at UCL. Her research interests include ubiquitous computing and interaction design, particularly how to design interactive technologies that can augment and extend everyday learning and work activities. Central to her work is a critical stance toward how visions, theories, and frameworks shape the fields of HCI, cognitive science, and Ubicomp. Rogers has been instrumental in promulgating new theories, alternative methodologies, and far-reaching research agendas (e.g. "Being Human: HCI in 2020" manifesto).

Yvonne Rogers with Helen Sharp (center) and Jennifer Preece (right) at their book party at the ACM CHI Conference on Human Factors in Computing Systems in Vancouver, BC, Canada in 2011.

Colleagues in the field of HCI recognize Rogers for her wide range of contributions to the field, from her

Ph.D. work on iconic interfaces to her recent work on public displays and behavioral change. She has also developed several influential theoretical frameworks, including external cognition, and pioneered an approach to innovation and ubiquitous learning.

From 2000–2007, Rogers contributed to the UK Equator Project as a principal investigator. The interdisciplinary research collaboration aimed to explore the relationship between the physical and the digital for a range of user experiences, including playing and learning. Part of the project involved a study called Ambient Wood, which encouraged children to explore biological processes in a forest using wirelessly connected probing devices. The researchers noted that the children readily learned and began to use the new technology to explore the woods in collaborative, imaginative ways.

Brad Myers presents Rogers with her award as a newly elected member of the CHI Academy at the ACM CHI Conference on Human Factors in Computing Systems in May 2012 in Austin, TX.

Rogers has authored or contributed to more than 250 publications, including the bestselling textbook *Interaction Design; Beyond Human-Computer Interaction*, which has been translated into six languages. She has served on various conference committees and advisory boards and is a Fellow of the British Computer Society. She was also awarded a prestigious EPSRC dream fellowship concerned with rethinking the relationship between aging, computing, and creativity. SIGCHI elected Rogers to the CHI Academy in 2012 and made a Fellow of the ACM in 2017.

Affiliations:

➢ Professor of HCI, Computing Department, Open University (2006–2011)

➢ Professor in Informatics, Indiana University (2003–2006)

➢ Professor, School of Cognitive and Computing Sciences, Sussex University (1992–2003)

Links:

➢ Homepage

➢ Wikipedia

MARY BETH ROSSON
PSYCHOLOGY AND SOFTWARE ENGINEERING AUTHORITY

Mary Beth Rosson has a long research history that includes object-oriented software engineering, collaborative learning, online communities, scenario-based design, and HCI theory development. Her software engineering side is strong on user evaluation, such as her work in the End Users to Shape Effective Software (EUSES) Consortium. She's been a devoted contributor to the SIGCHI community, including chairing the SIGCHI 2007 Conference.

– Ben Shneiderman

Mary Beth Rosson is a Professor of Information Sciences and Technology at the Pennsylvania State University. She was among the earliest researchers to study the psychological issues associated with the object-oriented paradigm, and she spent many years developing and evaluating object-oriented tools for professional programmers. She studies the interplay between the concerns of HCI and software engineering in addition to the tools and practices of end-user developers in educational and general business contexts.

Mary Beth Rosson with John Carroll at the ACM CHI Conference on Human Factors in Computing Systems in Minneapolis, MN, April 20–25, 2002.

Prior to joining the School of Information Sciences and Technology at Penn State in 2003, Rosson was a professor of computer science at Virginia Tech for 10 years and a research staff member and manager at IBM's T. J. Watson Research Center for 11 years.

She actively participates in the ACM SIGCHI community, including serving as the General Chair for the ACM CHI Conference on Human Factors in Computing Systems in 2007. She authored *Usability Engineering: Scenario-Based Development of Human-Computer Interaction* as well as many other articles, book chapters, and tutorials.

Donald Norman, Mary Beth Rosson, Stuart Card, and Eric Bergman at the ACM CHI Conference on Human Factors in Computing Systems in Minneapolis, MN, April 20–25, 2002.

Rosson was awarded the SIGCHI award for service as CHI 1997 Technical Program Co-Chair International and the ACM Recognition of Service award in 2001. In 2007, she was recognized as a Distinguished Scientist by the ACM.

Affiliations:

➤ Associate Dean for Graduate and Undergraduate Studies, College of Information Sciences and Technology, Pennsylvania State University, (2015–Present)

➤ Interim Dean, College of Information Sciences and Technology, Penn State University, (2014–2015)

➤ Associate Dean for Undergraduate Studies, College of Information Sciences and Technology, Penn State University, (2012–2014)

➤ Professor, College of Information Sciences and Technology, Penn State University, (2003–Present)

Links:

➤ Homepage

➤ Wikipedia

BEN SHNEIDERMAN
PIONEER OF DIRECT MANIPULATION

I'm a bit uncomfortable to include myself in this collection, but I'd be uncomfortable leaving myself out. The photos of me were often taken by the people who were wondering why I was taking their pictures—in the days before widespread use of cellphone cameras, taking candid photos was often seen with suspicion. My subjects wanted to take my photo, which I was happy enough to have, especially those that show me interacting with others. So I thank all those who have contributed to my own history album.

– Ben Shneiderman

Ben Shneiderman has worked in HCI for nearly half a century. While still a doctoral student, Shneiderman and research partner Isaac Nassi devised a practical graphic to represent programming structure (similar to a flowchart). The Nassi-Shneiderman diagram proved so successful, it was adopted as an international standard in 1985.

His most visible work is what we know today as hyperlinks—highlighted, clickable links embedded in text and graphics. The hyperlinks were a natural application of his theory of direct manipulation, as were the small touchscreen keyboards, now used in billions of smartphones. Shneiderman's information visualization research served as the basis for Spotfire, a highly successful commercial product. He was an early researcher in the growing field of universal usability, which strives to provide equal access to technology for diverse populations.

Tom Furness, Ben Shneiderman, Jennifer Preece, and Andrew Sears at the ACM CHI Conference on Human Factors in Computing Systems in Seattle, WA on April 1, 2001.

His 1986 book, *Designing the User Interface: Strategies for Effective Human-Computer Interaction*, appeared in 6th edition in 2016. In recent years, Shneiderman has focused on improving information visualization in business, medical, and social media enterprises with projects such as treemaps, NodeXL (for network data), and EventFlow (for event sequences).

Ben Shneiderman receiving his SIGCHI Achievement Award and membership to the CHI Academy at the ACM CHI Conference on Human Factors in Computing Systems in Seattle, WA, March 31–April 5, 2001.

Shneiderman is a member of the U.S. National Academy of Engineering and a Fellow of the AAAS, ACM, IEEE, National Academy of Inventors, and SIGCHI Academy. He has received six honorary doctorates in recognition for his research.

Affiliations:

- ➤ Professor (1989–Present), Founding Director of the Human-Computer Interaction Lab (1983–2000), Associate Professor (1979–1989), Assistant Professor (1976–1979), University of Maryland
- ➤ Assistant Professor, Department of Computer Science, Indiana University (1973–1976)

Links:

- ➤ Homepage
- ➤ Wikipedia

JOHN C. THOMAS
PSYCHOLOGY AND COMPUTER SCIENCE AUTHORITY

My admiration for John goes back to the early 1980s. His fresh way of looking made me pay attention. John's story-telling and writing skills were also inspirational examples as in his early understanding of the role of metaphor in HCI design. I sometimes thought his ideas were unrealizable, such as his 1999 Million Person Communities, but he successfully anticipated social networks that were much bigger. John and Wendy Kellogg came under the influence of the Younger Next Year *book, becoming exercise devotees, which definitely changed my behavior.*

– Ben Shneiderman

John C. Thomas currently does independent consulting in HCI and writes both fiction and non-fiction. After receiving his Ph.D. in psychology from the University of Michigan in 1971, Thomas managed the "Mental Performance and Aging" research project, for which he designed hardware, software, and interfaces for online testing and analysis. This work resulted in the "Organism-Environment Interaction Theory of Aging." In 1973, Thomas began work at the IBM T.J. Watson Research Center, where he researched several areas of HCI. He spent two years at IBM CHQ in the Chief Scientist's Office advocating for IBM to pay more attention to the human aspects of their products. He left IBM in 1986 to found and direct the Artificial Intelligence Laboratory at NYNEX Science and Technol-

Thomas with Jerry Weinberg (left) and Michael Schneider (right) at the first Conference on Human Factors in Computing Systems in Gaithersburg, MD in 1982.

ogy, where he established world-class groups in applied expert systems, speech recognition, neural networks, and HCI before returning to IBM.

Wendy Kellogg and John C. Thomas at the CHI 2011 Conference in Vancouver, BC Canada in May 2011.

From 1998–2013, he conducted HCI research at IBM's T. J. Watson Research Center and helped formulate IBM strategies for Cognitive Computing, Smart Cities and IT for the Next Billions. Projects included the development of a socio-technical pattern language, the business uses of stories, High Performance Computing tools, and the "Dynamic Learning Environment" project, which won several best paper awards and the 2004 Brandon Hall Gold Prize for technical innovation in e-learning.

Thomas played an active role in the formation of SIG-CHI, ACM's Special Interest Group in Computer Human Interaction. He served as publications co-chair for the Gaithersburg Conference. He was general co-chair of CHI in 1991. He also served on the SIGCHI Conference Management Committee from 1992–1995 and on the SIGCHI Executive Committee from 2009–2015. He has co-chaired many workshops on HCI patterns and socio-technical patterns at CHI, CSCW, ECSCW, and INTERACT.

Thomas is credited with more than 250 publications and invited presentations in HCI, computer science, and psychology. He served on numerous Ph.D. committees as well as grant review committees for NSF, DARPA, ONR, and SBIR. With Wendy Kellogg, he developed and delivered the training materials for IBM's World Jam, the first very large-scale on-line real time collaboration. He currently manages a LinkedIn group called HCI/UX Mentoring Circle.

Affiliations:

➤ Research Staff Member (2001–Present); Manager, Knowledge Socialization (1998–2001), IBM Research

➤ Executive Director, Bell Atlantic Science and Technology (1997–1998)

➤ Executive Director (1994–1997); Director, Artificial Intelligence Laboratory (1986–1993), NYNEX Science and Technology

Links:

➤ Truthtable.com

MARILYN "MANTEI" TREMAINE
"FOUNDING MOTHER" OF SIGCHI

Marilyn Mantei's pioneering contributions helped develop the fields of collaborative technologies. She showed the way forward with theories, real systems, and testing in large corporations with real users. She also gave generously of her time and energy to get SIGCHI going, and then did the hard work of developing educational programs and curricula.

– Ben Shneiderman

Marilyn "Mantei" Tremaine is widely regarded as one of the earliest and most prominent leaders in the field of HCI. During her distinguished career, Tremaine pioneered the application of digital media to a variety of problems, served as a mentor to multiple generations of students, and contributed to foundation of the ACM's Special Interest Group on Computer-Human Interaction (SIGCHI), the premier international society for professionals, academics, and students with a shared interest in human-technology and HCI.

Marilyn "Mantei" Tremaine, Michael Schneider, and David Beard at the ACM CHI Conference on Human Factors in Computing Systems in San Francisco, CA on April 14, 1985.

Tremaine's educational background combined several disciplines, including business, cognitive psychology, computer science, and sociology. During her two years at CMU, Allen Newell had a significant impact on her understanding of HCI. This interdisciplinary background served her well as she made a career in HCI. As an assistant professor at the University of Michigan, Tremaine conducted research on Database Interfaces and the integration of HCI into software engineering while teaching courses in Information Systems, networking, HCI, and decision support systems. During her time at Rutgers University, Tremaine developed and led a new Masters in Business Science degree, User Experience Design (UXD). The program uniquely prepares its students for careers in HCI through multiple projects, ample one-on-one mentoring, and frequent guest lectures from professionals in the field.

Marilyn "Mantei" Tremaine with Elliot Cole at the ACM Conference on Assistive Technologies (ASSETS) in Arlington, VA on November 14, 2000.

In 2005, Tremaine received the CHI Lifetime Service Award, recognizing her contributions to the foundation and growth of SIGHCI. As "founding mother" of SIGCHI and the CHI conferences, Tremaine was active in all early CHI conferences, served as a member of various SIGCHI committees, and chaired the CHI 86, CSCW 92, and ASSETS conferences. She served as President of SIGCHI from 1998–2002.

Since retiring in 2014, Tremaine has pursued her love for cooking through her entrepreneurial project, M3 Catering. She began volunteering to cater cocktail receptions for former U.S. Representative for New Jersey Rush D. Holt, Jr. in 2012 and has expanded to offering catering services to other candidates in the Democratic Party, including Bonnie Watson Coleman, New Jersey's first African American female Representative to Congress.

Affiliations:

- ➤ Chief Cook, M3 Catering (2012–Present)

- ➤ Head of User Experience Design Masters Degree (2009–2014), Research Professor (1997–2014), Rutgers University

- ➤ Vice President, Usability NJ (2008–2011)

- ➤ Co-Founder and President (1998–2002), ACM-SIGCHI

Links:

- ➤ Rutgers Faculty Profile

- ➤ Wikipedia

ANDY VAN DAM
GRAPHICS GURU

Andries van Dam has taught a remarkable number of students who have gone on to successful careers, especially as chairs of computer science departments. He is much appreciated by his students and colleagues like me for his intensity, emotional connectedness, and professional generosity. His devotion to 3D technology and user interfaces led to the highly influential book, Fundamentals of Interactive Computer Graphics, written with James Foley in 1980, with later editions in English and other languages. He's also rightly proud of his five-decade-long effort on hypertext/hypermedia systems.

– Ben Shneiderman

Andries "Andy" van Dam's work focuses on interactive media, from computer graphics to hypermedia, particularly for educational purposes. He is a leader in work on electronic books with interactive illustrations.

Van Dam at the ACM CHI Conference on Human Factors in Computing Systems in Boston, MA in 1994.

With Ted Nelson, Van Dam designed both HES and FRESS, the first and second hypertext systems that allowed separate pages of text to be connected via hyperlinks, such as this one.

Also a star educator in the field of computer graphics, Van Dam helped write the industry standard instructional textbook in computer graphics, *Computer Graphics: Principles and Practice*, with James D. Foley, Steven

K. Feiner, and J. F. Hughes. He is a member of the National Academy of Engineering, has received the ACM SIGGRAPH Steven Anson Coons Award for Outstanding Creative Contributions to Computer Graphics in 1991 and is a member of the SIGGRAPH Academy.

Andy Van Dam (second from left) at Asana Restaurant in Boston, MA, with Ben Shneiderman (l), Aaron Marcus, and Ron Baecker, celebrating Aaron's election to the CHI Academy. April 5, 2009.

Affiliations:

➢ Microsoft Research Technical Advisory Board (1991–2006)

➢ Chairman, Computing Research Association (1985–1987)

➢ Co-Founder and innaugural chair, Department of Computer Science, Brown University (1979–1985)

➢ Co-Founder ACM SIGGRAPH (1967)

➢ Faculty, Brown University (1965–Present)

Links:

➢ Homepage

➢ Wikipedia

JIMMY WALES
FOUNDER OF WIKIPEDIA

While Jimmy Wales is not really an HCI researcher, his development of Wikipedia has had an enormous impact on user experiences. I've greatly admired his thoughtful work over the past two decades in developing the energetic Wikipedia community with its devotion to giving free access to the world's information to all people in their own languages. The Wikimania conferences produced among the most enjoyable professional encounters I've had, with devoted contributors eagerly sharing their ideas and working through the challenges of making Wikipedia even more successful.

– Ben Shneiderman

Jimmy Wales is an Internet entrepreneur best known as the founder of Wikipedia, the now ubiquitous free collaborative online encyclopedia, and the Wikimedia Foundation. In 2000, Wales' vision of "free knowledge for free minds" inspired him to create Nupedia, a free encyclopedia featuring an extensive peer-review process to ensure quality. When Wales added a collection of web pages called "wikis" to enable anyone with access to contribute and modify content, the project was renamed Wikipedia. Wikipedia's success contributed to the rise of a trend in web development called Web 2.0, which aims to foster creativity, collaboration, and sharing among users. As Wikipedia expanded, Wales became its spokesperson and promoter through media appearances and speaking engagements. *TIME Magazine* named Wales one of its "100 Most Influential People" in the "Scientists and Thinkers" category in 2006 for his work with Wikipedia.

Wales presents at the Wikimania 2012 conference at George Washington University in Washington, D.C. in July 2012.

Wales with Dan Bricklin (left) and Mitch Kapor (center) at Wikimania 2006, the second annual international Wikimedia conference, at the Harvard Law School campus in Cambridge, MA in August 2006.

In 2003, Wales founded the Wikimedia Foundation, a nonprofit organization promoting the growth, development, and distribution of free, multilingual content to the public. The following year, Wales and Angela Beesley co-founded the for-profit company Wikia, Inc., a collection of wikis on various subjects all hosted on a single website. The World Economic Forum named Wales one of the "Young Global Leaders" of 2007, recognizing him among the top 250 young leaders across the world who achieved significant professional accomplishments and demonstrated their commitment to society and potential to contribute to the shaping of the future world. Wales continues to dedicate his time to promoting free speech and Internet freedom. He has said, "Imagine a world in which every single person on the planet is given free access to the sum of all human knowledge. That's what we're doing."

Affiliations:

- ➤ Board Member, Creative Commons (Present)

- ➤ Advisory Board Member, Sunlight Foundation (Present)

- ➤ Advisory Board Member, MIT Center for Collective Intelligence (Present)

- ➤ Fellow, Berkman Center for Internet and Society at Harvard Law School (Present)

- ➤ Chairman emeritus, Wikimedia Foundation (2006–Present)

- ➤ President of Wikia, Inc. (2004–Present)

Links:

- ➤ Homepage

- ➤ Wikipedia

- ➤ Encyclopaedia Britannica

TERRY WINOGRAD
COMPUTER INNOVATOR WITH A FOCUS ON PEOPLE

Terry Winograd began his career with a highly influential dissertation, "Understanding Natural Language," in which he demonstrated success in dealing with a limited set of nouns and verbs related to his "blocks world." I wrote critically about the utility of this work in my 1980 book Software Psychology, *so I was pleased that Winograd's 1987 book with Flores,* Understanding Computers and Cognition, *reported that "computers can't understand natural language." I called him up to discuss and found that he was recommending my critique to his students. From then on, we developed a warm, collegial relationship. I looked forward to my Stanford visits and chances to speak for his famed HCI course. I always admired Terry for his deep understanding of ethical issues in computing, his activism through the Computer Professionals for Social Responsibility, and his efforts to promote HCI at Stanford. His masterful lectures were always an attraction for me, as was his clear thinking about research and social issues. He famously worked with Sergei Brin and Larry Page to write the key paper that was the basis for Google. More than most of my colleagues, he was a model and inspiration to me, and to many others.*

– Ben Shneiderman

Terry Winograd is a Professor Emeritus of Computer Science at Stanford University, where he founded the Stanford Human-Computer Interaction Group and was one of the founders of the Hasso Plattner Institute for Design (d.school). Winograd is recognized in the fields of AI and the philosophy of mind for his work with natural language using the SHRDLU program. The program, which Winograd wrote as his Ph.D. thesis at MIT in the late 1960s, aimed to provide computers with sufficient "understanding" to use natural language—language human beings would use to communicate. After focusing his early academic career on programming computers to interact with people as if they were other people, Winograd redirected his efforts to creating computer interactions that would support and enhance human experience. In his book, *Understanding Computers and Cognition*, written with Fernando Flores, he examined the underlying assumptions of symbolic AI, and argued that they were not adequate as a basis for intelligence.

Winograd talks with Tora Bikson at the ACM CHI Conference on Human Factors in Computing Systems in Atlanta, GA in March 1997.

Throughout his career, the common thread in all his work is the principle that technology invention must begin with and be shaped by an understanding of how technology affects people's lives and experiences. Winograd was a founder of the Computer Professionals for Social Responsibility, was elected to the CHI Academy in 2004, was elected as an ACM Fellow in 2009, and received the 2011 ACM SIGCHI Lifetime Research Award, recognizing him as "a major influence in HCI through broadening its perspectives, demonstrating the relevance and importance of diverse schools of thought to understanding and designing interaction.

Winograd with his SIGCHI Lifetime Achievement Award (upside down) at the ACM CHI Conference on Human Factors in Computing Systems in Vancouver, BC, Canada in 2011.

Affiliations:

➤ Faculty Member, Computer Science Department, Stanford University (1973–2013), Emeritus (2014–Present)

➤ Vice-chair, Bend the Arc: a Jewish Partnership for Justice (on national board 2015–Present)

➤ Co-director, Stanford Project on Liberation Technology (2009–2014)

➤ Consultant, Google (2001–2008)

Links:

➤ Wikipedia

Author Biography

Ben Shneiderman (http://www.cs.umd.edu/~ben) is a Distinguished University Professor in the Department of Computer Science, Founding Director (1983–2000) of the Human-Computer Interaction Laboratory (http://hcil.umd.edu), and a Member of the UM Institute for Advanced Computer Studies (UMIACS) at the University of Maryland. He is a Fellow of the AAAS, ACM, IEEE, and NAI, and a Member of the National Academy of Engineering, in recognition of his pioneering contributions to HCI and information visualization. His innovative contributions include the web's highlighted link that makes it easy for billions of users to get the information they want and the tiny touchscreen keyboard on mobile devices used around the world. His theories, research methods, and software tools have become popular topics in computer science, while revolutionizing the ways people use technology to improve their lives. He has received six honorary doctorates.

Shneiderman's recent books are *Designing the User Interface: Strategies for Effective Human-Computer Interaction* (6th ed., 2016) and *The New ABCs of Research: Achieving Breakthrough Collaborations* (2016).

Printed in the United States
by Baker & Taylor Publisher Services